LUMMI ISLAND COOKING

BLAINE WETZEL

PRESTEL

Munich • London • New York

28

46

60

72

80

90

104

118

138

156

184

FOR DANIELA!

Duh! The biggest inspiration in my life, the best chef ever, the funniest comedian of all time, and the most beautiful girl I have ever seen. She encouraged me to make this book and makes me the happiest man in the world every day.

INTRODUCTION
BLAINE WETZEL

First of all, I feel grateful.

Over the past ten years, I have been able to cook in what I believe to be the most ideal situation for a chef. When I started cooking in a little restaurant in Iowa, I never thought that my view of a grocery store parking lot would one day turn into the most beautiful sunsets, bright green trees, sparkly, shining water surrounded by mountains, and, occasionally, a few families of whales, seals, and soaring eagles passing by. And the local ingredients are as unbelievable as the landscapes. Since arriving on Lummi Island, I have worked to create a dream restaurant for both our team and our guests. The Willows Inn has slowly evolved in that time, but even as we make changes, we always maintain the integrity of this hundred-year-old inn.

This island is such a special place, with overwhelming natural beauty, that it still takes my breath away every day. It is full of century-old apple and stone-fruit orchards and small farms with carefully tended livestock, all cherished and supported by the small local community. The Willows Inn farm, Loganita Farm, provides us with ingredients that have been handpicked and nurtured from seed, and foragers on the island find amazing collections of mushrooms, blossoms, and nuts that continue to surprise me. The surrounding sea provides a vast array of fish and shellfish that offer flavors you can't find anywhere else. There is a rich history of craftsmanship here and talented Native and local artisans that create handmade utensils, knives, and stunning pottery that help us showcase those ingredients. All of these dedicated people and perfect surroundings come together to create the magic that is The Willows Inn.

Most people explore Lummi Island when they come to The Willows for the first time, driving around to see the sights before finding their way to the restaurant. I always want the menu to be the same: an exploration of the flavors of the island.

My style of cooking, the menus at The Willows Inn, and to some extent, the recipes in this book are all a snapshot of a moment in time on the island, a culinary reflection of this place, through my eyes, on any given day. That is what we share with our guests with every dish. These recipes are created to showcase the natural flavors of our ingredients. We cook with ingredients almost exclusively from Lummi Island and many of the flavors that make the restaurant unique start from a pantry of seasonings that we create, from vinegars and salts to sauces, ferments, and dried spices.

Each day, I like the menu to be a dramatic description of the island, grouping dishes into movements, series, or spreads that fill the table and share a theme. For instance, in the fall, during the height of mushroom season, I often serve four or five types of wild mushrooms, cooked similarly, to showcase the subtle and natural variations in their tastes and textures. Or, I will repeat the same presentation and technique with completely different ingredients to highlight their specific characteristics. Formatting the menu like this allows me to celebrate the families of ingredients that are in season at the same time and breaks up the menu in a way that's similar to songs on an album.

It wouldn't be possible to produce many of the dishes on our menu or in this book without Loganita Farm, which allows us to grow many of the specialty ingredients included. With their supremely skilled team, which has worked with me since day one, we have been able to build a farm program that supports the operations of the restaurant in a way that is nearly unmatched elsewhere. We are able to choose the best seed varieties and harvesting techniques, and adjust the size and flavor of the ingredients for each specific dish.

The rush of inspiration that comes each morning, when the farm order arrives, freshly pulled from the ground and still warm from the sun, is hard to describe. The smell, the feeling of snapping off a leaf, or the flash of freshness after taking a bite—these are the sensations that I love to share.

As our farm manager, Mary, always says, "a farmer's best year is their next year," and that has proven to be true! While our restaurant and inn have grown over the years, so has the farm. We've expanded the team and grounds to include a second plot that allows us to grow varieties that need more time and space, or those that take several years to harvest. Heated water lines help bring spring to our seed houses a little earlier in the year and warm hoop houses help us extend the warmth of summer just a bit longer.

Each year at the farm builds on the last, and the outline for the menu really begins with the land. We always want to have new menus and dishes from one year to the next and that starts with growing different plants at the farm. But we don't want to just guess which new plants might taste good, so we are constantly planting the farm with experimental varieties and testing for next year's menu. Everything we grow is an heirloom or an unusual variety that you rarely see elsewhere. Seed breeders make next year's seeds available in January, and the rare heirloom seeds we use sell out immediately to preorders, which means we have to plan essentially a year in advance and place our orders early. Think about that: all seeds for the entire year ordered by January.

In November, we review all the plants we grew at the farm that year, critiquing each and deciding on the experimental types for the next year. We have to plan the farm foot by foot, week by week, before the year even starts. This is when the menu is born: a rough outline of what we'll serve is created before the year even begins. We plant the farm with specific dishes in mind so that all of the ingredients for a recipe coincide and are available at the same time.

With experience, we have even learned to time the planting and harvesting of vegetables to coincide with the seasons for different fish and shellfish. It doesn't get much better than the first tuna of the season arriving the same day as the first caraflex cabbage is brought in from the farm and we're able to put our albacore and cabbage dish on the menu that very night.

Choosing, growing, and tasting new plant varieties can be like traveling to different parts of the world and even through time. It has been an amazing part of being a chef and something that I never expected. At the very foundation of different cuisines are the specific plant varieties from those parts of the world. The contrast in flavors, textures, and appearances between an Asian variety of cucumber and a Middle Eastern one is transporting, and there are hundreds more examples of that. Having my own farm has opened up a world of flavors and ingredients that I never knew existed, even as a trained chef. The varieties of herbs, berries, and vegetables that are commonly available only scratch the surface of what exists.

Being able to explore the world through our farm has been one of the most exciting aspects of my career. My wife, and the most talented chef, Daniela Soto-Innes, also has her own section to grow Mexican vegetables, herbs, and peppers for her to use in the kitchen. And yes, her cooking is way better than mine.

Without a doubt, the largest factor in our success is our team of talented chefs and service members from all over the world. Anyone who is interested in food or restaurants cannot help but be inspired by The Willows Inn. It is a very uncommon restaurant and I am lucky to work with the best and brightest of the industry who bring this special place to life. A chance to work in the most idyllic setting and be truly connected to our menu, our ingredients, our guests, and the island in the most fun and creative way is a joy I love to share. The Willows Inn is only possible because of this team of passionate individuals that works endlessly to present the very best version of Lummi Island to our guests each day.

And, also, the schedule—OMG!!!! The three months of the year that The Willows Inn is closed for winter is very unusual in the restaurant world and it has been so important to keeping the whole team fresh and inspired.

Our extended family, especially our artisan suppliers, are the other key to our success. Our passionate fishermen and foragers, ceramicists and artists, are relentless in getting us the best that the region has to offer. Many times, we work with only one person for a particular product or ingredient and over the years, we have developed access to a quality that is unavailable otherwise.

Our fish and shellfish are often delivered, straight off the fishing boat, to the beach in front of the restaurant. When the boat returns after days on the ocean, the kitchen always brims with excitement to see what our fisherman has found for us. He takes the time to process all of our fish using the Japanese ikejime technique to ensure the best possible texture. We actually have trouble with fish being too fresh and have to wait for it to relax for a day before it's ready to be cooked.

The fishermen of Lummi Island also practice the most sustainable form of salmon fishing possible. Developed by the Lummi people, reefnet fishing is a method of drawing salmon to the surface without stress or bycatch. Reefnet boats bring thousands of handpicked sockeye salmon to the restaurant each summer, and to me, the sensation of biting into the smoked sockeye salmon we serve at The Willows Inn is one of the best things on earth.

The ingredients of this area mean more to the Lummis than any of us. Their knowledge and traditional practices have provided amazing insight into how to utilize wild ingredients from the island. The ancestral techniques required to cook with skunk cabbage or the different local seaweeds are not easily found on YouTube, so being invited to observe important ceremonies and festivals has been incredibly inspiring to me and the staff here at The Willows Inn. In fact, we often use traditional Lummi recipes for initial inspiration or direction in how to approach the wild plants here on the island.

This book is an attempt to capture the result of all of this, what we do daily at The Willows Inn. I have arranged this book into sections and it loosely follows the format of the menu at the restaurant. Our menu changes dramatically throughout the seasons and from year to year. By formatting the menu into series of dishes with similar themes, we change significant portions of the menu at the same time—it makes it fun to be a guest or to work at The Willows Inn. I never imagined that I would get the opportunity to work next to hundreds of the most dedicated people in our field, all of whom made it possible to grow The Willows Inn, brick by brick, into what is now our dream restaurant and one that has held my interest for a decade now.

That said, this book represents only a small portion of the dishes that we serve at The Willows Inn and is intended to showcase some of where we are right now and to share how I like to cook.

I continuously draw inspiration from Lummi and I hope it inspires you, too.

A NOTE FROM THE FARM
MARY VON KRUSENSTIERN

Farm Manager
Loganita Farm, Lummi Island

Loganita is a one-acre, organic farm solely dedicated to growing ingredients for The Willows Inn on Lummi Island. Located a half mile from the restaurant, the farm perches above Rosario Strait, on a fertile piece of open land, protected by groves of trees. Our close proximity to the restaurant allows us to deliver vibrant produce to The Willows Inn kitchen multiple times each day: fresh herbs, specialty greens, and colorful winter squash delivered from the farm early in the morning are on a guest's plate that same night.

We work closely with The Willows Inn chefs throughout the year and at the end of each season, we sit down and review what worked well, and what didn't. We talk about produce we needed more or less of and discuss what we'd like to do differently to continue to evolve both of our operations. The chefs always have menu ideas for the following season, and we aim to translate those concepts into a tangible crop plan that makes their vision for the next season possible. The close relationship between the farm and the kitchen gives the chefs a degree of control and specificity over the produce they serve and informs the artistry of each and every course at The Willows.

At the farm, almost exclusively, we grow unique varieties of produce—tiny alpine strawberries, succulent ice plant, gray-blue oyster leaf, sturdy stalks of celtuce, and additional varieties we can't wait to try—and this is thanks to working with very select seed companies. Most of the produce we grow is so unusual, and harvested with such a degree of specificity for sizing, flavor, and more, that The Willows simply would not be able to source a similar product from a standard farm stand or larger supplier.

Each farm day begins with a daily harvest comprised of a variety of tender herbs, greens, and sensitive crops that need to be picked daily to ensure freshness. We work off of a punch sheet from the kitchen that's based on the specific dishes that will be on the dinner menu that evening. The farmers start harvesting early in the morning and deliver to The Willows midday then watch as the chefs open the bins and get right to work prepping the ingredients that will inform the prix fixe menu that evening.

After our delivery, we get down to the work of farming: planting, cultivating, laying drip line, replanting in the seed house and field, and all the tasks required to make the farm functional and abundant. In order to have a consistently diverse array of crops, we continuously plant seeds in the greenhouse and fields throughout the season. Over the course of the day, chefs visit the farm and walk the rows and we receive phone calls with subtle adjustments to their order. The success of our collaboration is borne out of continuous conversation and adaptation.

A successful farmer is always thinking ahead. As we harvest the last of a particular crop, we also deliver samples of what is nearly ready for harvest. The Willows Inn chefs are equally focused on the future and throw themselves into experiments for the next dish they're in the process of inventing. Much of what appears on the plate has been years in the making—the result of several seasons of vegetable trials, experiments, and conversations between the kitchen and farm.

Because we are at the mercy of nature, our annual plan always has an element of unpredictability: an early June rain challenges an eggplant crop, birds get the better of tiny seed sprouts, or we have a bumper crop of summer squash that comes into season a few weeks earlier than anticipated. As the farm adapts to these variables, the chefs fine tune the menu to reflect what is freshest, and in this process, the relationship between the restaurant and the farm continues to grow, develop, and streamline. Over the years, we've learned a lot about farming for a restaurant, as well as how to really utilize the farm well. We're constantly evolving what we do, both on the farm and in the restaurant, and look forward to many more delicious years of experimenting and collaborating between our teams.

ISLAND SERVICE

MEREDITH O'MALLEY
Restaurant Manager
The Willows Inn

As guests arrive on the property, their senses are heightened. They hear the soft crashing of the waves, birds soaring in the sky, the ambient noise of guests enjoying lunch on the deck. Facing east, they see The Willows tucked back into a wooded area surrounded by native landscaping and with smoke billowing out of the smokehouse. Turning their attention west, they'll notice a small chain of islands with the Canadian Cascades looking down upon them in the distance.

For most guests, a trip out to Lummi Island is a retreat—a retreat from the chaos of daily life, a time when their watches turn to island time as soon as they are crossing on the ferry. They take note of what makes Lummi Island special: our lack of a gas station or proper grocery store, wildlife sightings on the way to The Willows, narrow roads shared with pedestrians. All of it makes the island seem like a strange anomaly of reality, a place that more closely resembles the past. But most of all, guests notice the untouched beauty of the island and its surroundings.

The aesthetic and "feel" of the restaurant translates directly into our style of service, which is meant to be the perfect complement to the island's beauty and never a distraction from it. We avoid moving too quickly or overcrowding as to avoid causing any kind of alert. We don't deliver lengthy explanations of dishes. Instead, we share stories in an enthusiastic way to quench our guests' excitement, but not so much that it becomes overwhelming. Our conversations are never rushed but genuine and warm as if we're speaking with an old friend. Returning guests are comforted by familiar faces, year after year, but are pleased to meet new members of our family all the same.

We pair the menu with nearly all local wines. Even in the glass, guests can taste the efforts of the land and people in the region. Our cocktail program is a direct reflection of the island and takes advantage of farmed and foraged items. The phrase, "what grows together, goes together" truly epitomizes our approach to food and wine pairing.

The interior of the property resembles a home where people feel instantly comfortable. Our service style aims to share that same message. Familiar, warm, and at ease. Some guests arrive in suits and formal gowns, while others wear flip flops riddled with sand from their pre-dinner walk on the beach. Neither guest feels uncomfortable with their decision, as both are perfect attire for dinner on Lummi Island. For most, visiting Lummi is an anticipatory event that is often coupled with high expectations. The natural aesthetic of the island with its beautiful sunsets, the simple presentation of outstanding ingredients, and the relaxed nature of our service dance together to create a memorable experience for all.

FRESH FRUIT

The old fruit orchards are one of Lummi Island's most beautiful features, and all summer long the chefs' first task of the day is to go out and pick ripe fruit for that night.

Being able to pick the vegetables and fruits that you cook and serve that very evening gives us a larger purpose than simply cooking. It reminds us how lucky we are to be surrounded by so much nature, and nature that has been on the island for at least a century.

The orchards, nearby barns, and old rusty pickup trucks are like a scene from a movie set. To look out from the kitchen window and see tables set with ripe fruit, the sunset over the ocean, and the sun shining on the fruit, I can't help but smile for a while, and take it all in with a big breath, wishing I was a guest at one of those tables at that moment in time.

I will never forget running late and picking apples with Daniela just before dinner service and then rushing back to the kitchen where they were sliced and served right away. I am constantly reminded of how lucky I am to work in such an ideal setting.

I never expected to think of serving a piece of sliced fruit as some sort of accomplishment, but these simple dishes require all the skills of a trained chef and are as challenging to perfect as any recipe in this book.

We watch in anticipation, as the fruit ripens, beginning with those on the outer branches that are more exposed to the sun, and moving to the inner ones—waiting until they almost drip with sweetness, and then carefully transporting them to the kitchen.

Ripe fruit has to be handled with the lightest touch and the sharpest knife, carved perfectly, and at just the right temperature. A plate of fresh fruit can be such an expression of craft that it is safe to say that it is one of my favorite things to prepare and eat, even if it requires no cooking at all.

GREEN FIGS AND LEAF CREAM
SERVES 4

INGREDIENTS

10 large fig leaves, divided
270 ml grapeseed oil
1.15 liters heavy cream, divided
8 egg yolks
250 g sugar
10 green figs, cut into quarters

PREPARATION

Blend 2 large fig leaves with the grapeseed oil in a blender on high speed for 5 minutes and let infuse in the refrigerator overnight. Strain the oil and reserve.

Heat 500 ml of the heavy cream with the remaining 8 large fig leaves in a saucepan over medium until hot. Remove from the heat and let cool. Strain the cream and discard the fig leaves. Whisk the egg yolks with the fig leaf cream and sugar in the top of a double boiler (a large heat-safe bowl, covered and set over a pot of simmering water) until thickened, then let cool. Whip the remaining 650 ml of heavy cream to soft peaks and fold into the cooled custard.

TO COMPLETE

Spoon the fig leaf cream into 4 small bowls and top each with the fig leaf oil. Serve with the green figs.

MELONS AND LEMON VERBENA
SERVES 4

INGREDIENTS

4 melons, possible varieties include
    cantaloupe, Lemondrop, Prescott, or winter
25 ml verjus
20 lemon verbena leaves, torn into tiny pieces
2 flowering quinces, peeled, quartered,
    and finely grated

PREPARATION

Cut the melons in half and scrape out the seeds, reserving any melon juices. Scoop out the melon into evenly sized pieces and set in a large bowl. Reserve the hollow melon skins. Toss the melon chunks with the verjus, torn lemon verbena leaves, and grated quince and let marinate in the refrigerator for 1 hour.

TO COMPLETE

Arrange the marinated melon chunks in the hollow melon skins and finish with the fresh melon juices.

A BLACKBERRY STEW

SERVES 4

INGREDIENTS

500 g parsley leaves
500 g winter savory
540 ml grapeseed oil
250 g pickling lime
1 liter cold water
1 kg blackberries
250 g sugar
200 ml verjus
1 bunch fresh chamomile
1 bunch wood sorrel,
    leaves picked

PREPARATION

Blend the parsley leaves and winter savory with the grapeseed oil in a blender on high speed for 10 minutes. Cool and store the mixture in the refrigerator overnight. Strain and reserve the oil.

Dissolve the pickling lime with the cold water. Soak the blackberries overnight in this solution then rinse. Combine the blackberries, sugar, verjus, and chamomile in the top of a double boiler (a large heat-safe bowl, covered and set over a pot of simmering water) stirring occasionally, for 2 hours. Remove from the heat and discard the chamomile.

TO COMPLETE

Spoon the blackberries into 4 small bowls and top each with ¼ of the wood sorrel leaves and a spoonful of the herb oil.

STEAMED RHUBARB AND LEMON THYME

SERVES 4

INGREDIENTS

5 stalks rhubarb
150 ml simple syrup, divided
450 g lemon thyme leaves,
    divided, plus more for garnish
215 ml grapeseed oil
200 ml water
150 ml verjus

PREPARATION

FOR THE RHUBARB Trim the rhubarb and seal in a vacuum bag with 50 ml of the simple syrup then cook at 160°F (70°C) for 25 minutes. Remove the cooked rhubarb from the bag, reserving any cooking liquid. Cut the rhubarb into 4-inch (10 cm) segments then slice each segment into thin ribbons and brush with any reserved cooking liquid.

FOR THE LEMON THYME OIL Seal 20 g of the lemon thyme leaves with the grapeseed oil in a vacuum bag and cook at 175°F (80°C) for 1 hour then strain.

FOR THE LEMON THYME WATER Using a mortar and pestle, crush the remaining 430 g of lemon thyme leaves with the water, verjus, and the remaining 100 ml of simple syrup until a paste forms then strain.

TO COMPLETE

Place the rhubarb ribbons in 4 chilled bowls and cover each with the lemon thyme water. Finish with a drizzle of the lemon thyme oil and a few lemon thyme leaves.

MIXED WILD BERRIES
WITH ELDERFLOWERS
SERVES 4

INGREDIENTS

500 g fresh elderflowers (on the stem)
270 ml grapeseed oil
1 kg mixed wild berries

PREPARATION

Pick the elderflowers from the stems. Seal the
elderflower stems and ¾ of the flowers with the
grapeseed oil in a vacuum bag and cook at 175°F (80°C)
for 10 minutes. Juice half of the berries using
a cheesecloth then chill the juice and season with
the elderflower oil.

TO COMPLETE

Gently smash the remaining berries in the bottom
of 4 small bowls and cover with spoonfuls of both the
fresh berry juice and elderflower oil. Sprinkle with
the remaining fresh elderflowers.

SALMONBERRIES
WITH ELDERFLOWERS
SERVES 4

INGREDIENTS

500 g fresh elderflowers (on the stem)
270 ml grapeseed oil
1 kg salmonberries

PREPARATION

Pick the elderflowers from the stems. Seal the
elderflower stems and ¾ of the flowers with the
grapeseed oil in a vacuum bag and cook at 175°F (80°C)
for 10 minutes. Juice half of the berries using a
cheesecloth then chill the juice and season with the
elderflower oil.

TO COMPLETE

Gently smash the remaining berries in the bottom
of 4 small bowls and cover with spoonfuls of both the
fresh berry juice and elderflower oil. Sprinkle with
the remaining fresh elderflowers.

MARINATED FISHES

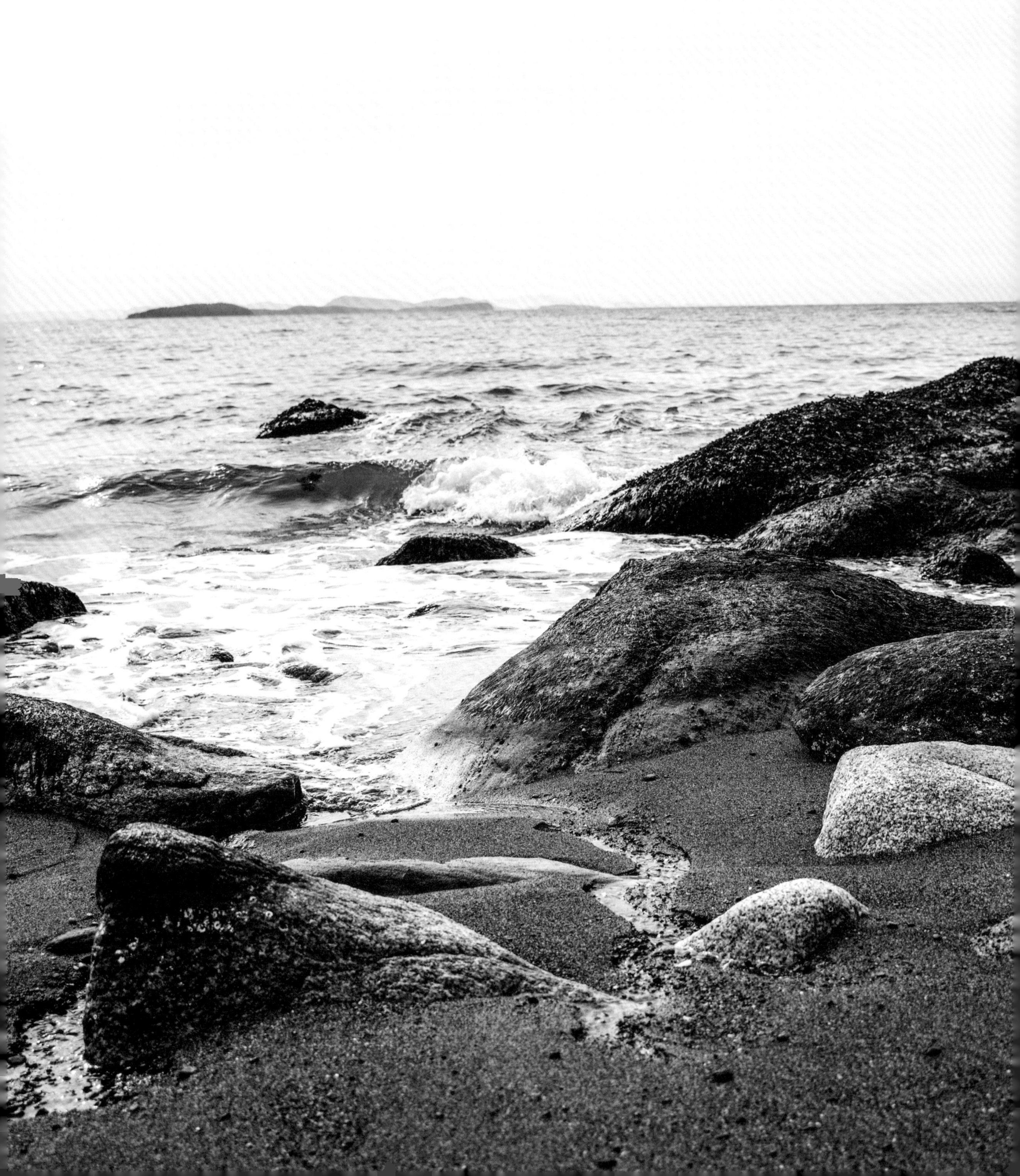

Ceviche might be my favorite way to eat fresh fish and shellfish.

I love the flavor and texture of seafood barely "cooked" by salt and acid. It is amazing how a quick marinade in a salty, acidic brine transforms fish and shellfish, making them brighter, fresher, and firmer.

Despite being a trained chef, I didn't know much about commercial fishing until I started to work directly with fishermen. In commercial fishing, many different types of fish are caught, but unfortunately, most are not worth keeping, because there is little to no market for them outside of selling them for pet food. Many taste incredible but are so delicate that they do not transport or store well. Some are too spiky or small to yield a reasonable fillet for the price, though they are otherwise delicious, while others are a little grainy at first but then turn beautifully velvety after being cured in a little salt.

Ceviche is a good way to work with these misfits, these abundant types of fish that are not commonly sought after and often accidentally caught. It also allows us to work with the freshest fish from around the island all year long. There are dozens of different types of rockfish, perch, snappers, and cod that live around the island and are almost never intended to be caught by fishermen or purchased by cooks, but with the right recipe, they can be every bit as incredible as the finest tuna belly.

We have a whole section of the menu dedicated to ceviche and different marinated fish and shellfish. These are some of the highlights from the last few years.

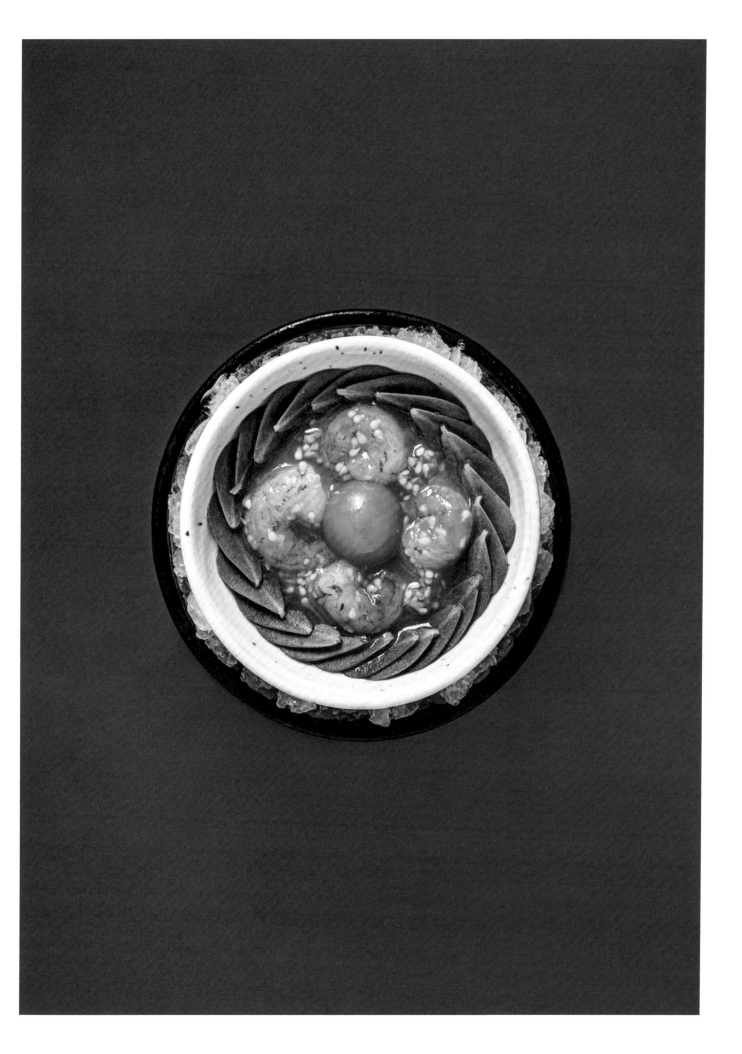

SEA URCHIN MARINATED IN TOMATO SEEDS
SERVES 4

INGREDIENTS

100 Sun Gold tomatoes
5 sea urchins
500 g purslane
50 ml olive oil

PREPARATION

FOR THE TOMATOES Setting aside 4 tomatoes, cut the rest in half, gently scrape against the flesh to remove and reserve all of the seeds and any juice, and discard the tomato flesh and skins.

FOR THE SEA URCHIN Remove the sea urchin tongues from the shell, clean, and marinate in a small amount of the tomato seeds, tomato juice, and a pinch of salt. Rest in the refrigerator for 6 hours or until firm. Reserve remaining tomato seeds and juice in refrigerator.

TO COMPLETE

Quarter the 4 reserved tomatoes and divide among 4 small bowls. Then, divide the sea urchin tongues among the bowls and arrange some of the purslane leaves around them. Cover with the remaining tomato seeds and drizzle with the olive oil.

STRIPED SHRIMP MARINATED IN TOMATO SEEDS
SERVES 4

INGREDIENTS

100 Sun Gold tomatoes
24 striped shrimp
500 g purslane
50 ml olive oil

PREPARATION

FOR THE TOMATOES Cut the tomatoes in half, gently scrape against the flesh to remove and reserve all of the seeds and any juice, and discard the tomato flesh and skins.

FOR THE STRIPED SHRIMP Remove the striped shrimp from the shells, clean, and marinate in a small amount of the tomato seeds, tomato juice, and a pinch of salt. Rest in the refrigerator for 6 hours or until firm.

TO COMPLETE

Divide the shrimp among 4 small bowls and arrange some of the purslane leaves around them. Cover with the remaining tomato seeds and drizzle with the olive oil.

SCALLOPS MARINATED IN CUCUMBER SEEDS

SERVES 4

INGREDIENTS

1 kg cucumbers
50 g fresh parsley seeds
50 g fresh dill seeds
10 g fresh fennel seeds
50 ml verjus
1 (25 g) piece fresh horseradish, peeled
10 sea scallops

PREPARATION

Cut the cucumbers in half, then remove and reserve the seeds and any juice, saving the cucumber pulp for another use. Using a mortar and pestle, grind the fresh parsley, dill, and fennel seeds with a pinch of salt and the verjus to make a paste. Grate the horseradish. Shuck the scallops then slice them into thick coins and lightly salt.

TO COMPLETE

Divide the scallop slices among 4 chilled bowls and cover each with a spoonful of the cucumber seeds and juice. Put a small pinch of the herb seed mixture and the grated horseradish on top of each slice of scallop.

TURNIPS MARINATED WITH SQUID

SERVES 4

INGREDIENTS

20 small squid
20 hakurei turnips
40 turnip greens
60 g caviar
50 ml olive oil

PREPARATION

Sauté the squid in a drizzle of grapeseed oil over medium-high heat until caramelized. Place the sautéed squid in a bowl, cover with aluminum foil, and let cool. Strain off and reserve any liquid that has accumulated in the bowl.

Boil the turnips in fresh seawater for 1 hour or until completely cooked. Drain and mash the cooked turnips and spread out on paper towels to absorb as much of the water as possible. In a mortar and pestle, smash the turnip greens into a paste.

TO COMPLETE

Place a small spoonful of the turnips, turnips greens, and caviar in each of 4 chilled bowls. Surround with the caramelized squid and squid juices and drizzle with olive oil.

NATIVE OYSTERS MARINATED IN WATERCRESS

SERVES 4

INGREDIENTS

FOR THE HORSERADISH OIL

1 (500 g) piece fresh
    horseradish, peeled
500 ml grapeseed oil

FOR THE WATERCRESS
PURÉE

1 kg watercress, leaves
    picked
270 ml grapeseed oil

FOR THE WATERCRESS
SAUCE

75 g watercress
25 g wheatgrass
300 ml ice cold water
10 ml verjus
20 Olympia oysters

PREPARATION

FOR THE HORSERADISH OIL Grate the fresh horseradish into the grapeseed oil and let infuse for 1 hour then strain.

FOR THE WATERCRESS PURÉE Blanch the watercress leaves for 4 minutes then shock them in ice water. Pack the leaves into a Pacojet canister, freeze, and process in the Pacojet 5 times. Whisk the blended watercress with the grapeseed oil to make a smooth purée.

FOR THE WATERCRESS SAUCE Blend the watercress, wheatgrass, and ice cold water in a blender on high speed for 20 to 30 seconds. Pass through a strainer and season with salt and the verjus.

TO COMPLETE

Shuck the oysters, rinse them in seawater, and pat dry. Brush the inside of 4 chilled bowls with the watercress purée and divide the oysters evenly among the bowls. Top each with a spoonful of the watercress sauce and a few drops of the horseradish oil.

ROCKFISH MARINATED WITH POBLANO PEPPERS

SERVES 4

INGREDIENTS

4 whole red rockfish
2 kg kosher salt, approximately
1 (200 g) piece ginger, peeled
325 ml grapeseed oil
225 g salt
10 liters water
20 poblano peppers

PREPARATION

FOR THE ROCKFISH Clean and scale the rockfish, then cut into 8 large fillets with the skin attached. Reserve all the bones for another use. In a shallow cake pan, completely cover the fillets with a heavy coating of kosher salt. Cure in the fridge for 24 hours, then rinse and pat dry the fillets. Quickly grill the skin side only over hot embers for 30 to 60 seconds then thinly slice.

FOR THE GINGER OIL Mince the ginger and cook with the grapeseed oil over low heat for 20 minutes. Strain and let cool.

FOR THE POBLANO FERMENT Dissolve the 225 g of salt in the water to create 2.25% brine. Chop the poblano peppers into 1-inch (2.5 cm) pieces, discarding the seeds and stems, then add the peppers to the salt brine. Set the brine aside in a warm place to ferment for 10 days then strain, reserving the liquid and discarding the peppers.

TO COMPLETE

Arrange a few slices of the cured rockfish in each of 4 chilled bowls and cover each with the poblano ferment liquid and the ginger oil.

SPOTTED PRAWNS MARINATED WITH NASTURTIUMS

SERVES 4

INGREDIENTS

15 spot prawns
5 stalks green rhubarb
35 g salt
200 g lovage flowers
215 ml grapeseed oil
45 sage blossoms
15 oregano blossoms
5 sage leaves
15 nasturtium leaves

PREPARATION

FOR THE PRAWNS Peel the prawns and cut the tails crosswise into 4 pieces. Juice 4 stalks of the rhubarb and combine 500 ml of the rhubarb juice with the salt to make a 7% brine. Add the prawns to the brine and marinate in the refrigerator for 6 hours.

FOR THE LOVAGE FLOWER OIL Seal the lovage flowers and grapeseed oil in a vacuum bag and cook at 175°F (80°C) for 1 hour, then strain and let cool.

TO COMPLETE

Peel and dice the remaining stalk of rhubarb and tear the sage blossoms, oregano blossoms, and sage leaves into small pieces. Put 4 pieces of prawn and some of the marinade in each nasturtium leaf and cover with the diced rhubarb and torn herbs. Finish with a drizzle of the lovage flower oil.

I have noticed that it doesn't matter if spring comes in early or late, rainy or hot. The season's fruits and vegetables grow in the same order. The first greens are from swamp (skunk) cabbage and cow parsley, while thimbleberries are always the first berries to ripen and salmonberries are second. It doesn't matter what temperature it is outside. I always know when spring's bounty is coming.

Vegetable dishes fill the menu all throughout spring and are, to me, the most gratifying to cook. After a long winter, seeing the first sprouts of what our spring greens and veggies are going to be is extremely exciting.

The first herbs and leaves taste incredible straight off the plant and can be transformed with just the slightest cooking and used together in endless combinations. Fresh greens can change from one week to the next and can be so different from one variety to another even though they look almost the same.

I will always remember my first taste of spring greens from Lummi Island. It was as if I had never eaten a salad before—I ate four big bowls and still wanted more. Crunching into crisp greens from the farm, there is a refreshing feeling of simplicity that connects me to nature in a completely unique way.

I never imagined that I would be in the kitchen saying, "Noooo! No salt! No acid! No seasoning!" It goes against everything I've ever learned, but it's also so apparent that the subtle flavors of these tender greens is easily lost with heavy seasoning—sometimes even a tiny sprinkle of salt mutes the nuances I want to highlight.

A CHILLED TURNIP SOUP
SERVES 4

INGREDIENTS

16 baseball-sized globe turnips
600 ml seawater
225 g turnip greens
100 ml extra-virgin olive oil

PREPARATION

FOR THE COOKED TURNIPS Peel 12 turnips completely to avoid any fibrous skin and chop into a rough medium dice. Place the turnips in 3 to 4 large vacuum bags, fill each bag with the seawater, and seal. Cook at 212°F (100°C) for 90 minutes or until the turnips are completely cooked and very soft. Cool bags in an ice bath then drain the solids in a fine-mesh strainer, pressing to remove any liquid. Discard the liquid and lay the solids on a baking sheet lined with enough paper towels to continue absorbing any excess liquid. Set aside.

FOR THE TURNIP GREENS Finely chop the turnip greens and muddle with a pinch of coarse salt in a mortar and pestle until a thick paste forms.

FOR THE TURNIP JUICE Peel and juice the remaining 4 turnips.

TO COMPLETE

Crush the cooked turnips with a fork to make a coarse mash. Mix the cooked turnips with the fresh turnip juice to make a thick soup. Fill 4 chilled bowls with the turnip soup and finish with a spoonful of the muddled turnip greens and a drizzle of the extra-virgin olive oil.

WILD BEACH PEA TIPS AND LOVAGE STEMS
SERVES 4

INGREDIENTS

1 kg yogurt
4 lovage stems
120 wild beach pea tips
25 ml grapeseed oil

PREPARATION

Hang the yogurt in cheesecloth set over a bowl and store overnight in the refrigerator. Collect the whey and reserve the strained yogurt for another use. Warm the whey in a small pan over low heat.

Peel the lovage stems and cut into thin slices.

TO COMPLETE

Toss the lovage stems and beach pea tips with the grapeseed oil and steam for 1 minute. Divide the lovage stems and beach pea tips among 4 bowls and mist with the warm whey.

A LEEK GRATIN

SERVES 4

INGREDIENTS

3 kg yogurt
10 leeks
780 g scallions
100 ml chicken glace
50 ml apple cider vinegar
50 ml grapeseed oil

PREPARATION

FOR THE WHEY Hang the yogurt in cheesecloth set over a bowl and store overnight in the refrigerator. Collect the whey and reserve the strained yogurt for another use.

FOR THE LEEKS Cut the leeks lengthwise in half and char in a skillet then add enough water to cover the leeks. Cover with a piece of parchment paper and gently cook over low heat until tender.

FOR THE SCALLION PURÉE Separate the scallion tops and bottoms then blanch the green tops and shock them in ice water. Grill the white scallion bottoms until charred and tender. Blend the chicken glace, apple cider vinegar, and charred white scallion bottoms in a blender on high speed until combined. Add the blanched green scallion tops and slowly drizzle in the 50 ml grapeseed oil, blending until smooth. Season the purée with salt and strain.

TO COMPLETE

Trim the cooked leeks, peeling off the outer layers and slicing them crosswise into 1 ¼-inch (3 cm) segments. Spoon some of the scallion purée into the bottom of 4 shallow bowls and cover with the leek slices. Finish with a spoonful of the whey and a drizzle of grapeseed oil.

THIN SLICES OF BEET WITH GIN

SERVES 4

INGREDIENTS

FOR THE YOGURT
500 g cow's milk yogurt
50 ml gin, such as Spy Hop
10 ml verjus
10 ml simple syrup

FOR THE LOVAGE
FLOWER OIL
200 g lovage flowers
215 ml grapeseed oil

FOR THE BEETS
2.4 kg all-purpose flour
1.6 liters water
800 g kosher salt
6 large red beets, peeled

FOR THE GARNISH
100 hazelnuts, skinned
50 dry lavender buds

PREPARATION

FOR THE GIN YOGURT Hang the yogurt in cheesecloth set over a bowl and store overnight in the refrigerator. Reserve the whey for another use. Mix the strained yogurt with the gin, verjus, and simple syrup and keep refrigerated.

FOR THE LOVAGE FLOWER OIL Seal the lovage flowers and grapeseed oil in a vacuum bag and cook at 175°F (80°C) for 1 hour then strain and keep refrigerated.

FOR THE BEETS Using a stand mixer with a paddle attachment, combine the flour, water, and salt until the ingredients are incorporated and the mixture is homogeneous. On a lightly floured work surface, roll out the dough until ¾-inch (2 cm) thick. Wrap each beet in the dough, covering completely, then transfer to a baking sheet and bake at 325°F (160°C) for 2 hours or until the beets are soft inside—check them by inserting a cake tester in the middle. Unwrap the beets and let cool then thinly slice and brush each slice with the lovage flower oil.

FOR THE GARNISH Toast the hazelnuts at 350°F (175°C) until dark then grind in a mortar and pestle into a coarse paste.

TO COMPLETE

Gently roll the sliced beets into loose rounds then brush with more of the lovage flower oil. Place dollops of the gin yogurt in each of the 4 bowls and arrange 5 of the beet rounds in each bowl, topping with small spoonfuls of the hazelnut paste. Sprinkle with a pinch of the lavender buds.

AN HERBED TOSTADA

SERVES 4

INGREDIENTS

FOR THE TEMPURA BATTER

300 g all-purpose flour

300 g rice flour

20 g lovage salt (see page 134)

20 g sugar

300 g kale, roughly chopped

400 ml water

200 ml sauerkraut brine

100 ml eggs, beaten

FOR THE OYSTER EMULSION

450 ml grapeseed oil

330 g shucked oysters

63 g parsley leaves

TO COMPLETE

24 large mustard green leaves

700 ml tempura batter

400 g oyster emulsion

Flowers: including but not limited to violas, nasturtiums, marigolds, bachelor buttons, and borage flowers

Herbs: including but not limited to mint, shiso, tarragon, oyster leaf, ice plant, nasturtium leaves, chervil, miner's lettuce, oxalis, French sorrel, wood sorrel, and lovage

PREPARATION

FOR THE TEMPURA BATTER In a large bowl, mix the all-purpose flour, rice flour, lovage salt, and sugar. Blend the kale, water, and sauerkraut brine in a blender on medium speed until smooth then pass through a fine-mesh strainer. Add the strained liquid and the beaten eggs to the flour mixture and combine well.

FOR THE OYSTER EMULSION Blend the grapeseed oil, oysters, and parsley leaves in a blender on high speed until smooth. Pass through a fine-mesh strainer, chill until cool, and season with salt.

TO COMPLETE

Trim each mustard green leaf into a tall diamond shape, measuring roughly 2 to 3 inches (5 to 7.5 cm) per side. Lightly batter each mustard green leaf and fry at 325°F (160°C) for 1 minute per side or until puffed and crispy. Let the fried mustard green leaves drain and cool on a paper towel–lined baking sheet. Spread a thick layer of the oyster emulsion on top of each fried mustard green leaf then tile the herbs and flowers onto each tostada, securing them by pressing the end of each leaf or flower into the emulsion.

SHELLFISH

Lummi is a small, nearly uninhabited island in the Pacific Northwest and it makes for one of the most beautiful restaurant settings on earth. The beaches and waters around the island are full of so much sea life and fresh shellfish that it's unlike anything I've ever seen or tasted.

But the main reason I decided to move to this almost-deserted island was because of how different and more delicious and precise everything tasted. It was like I didn't really know how crab, shrimp, clams, mussels, and oysters tasted until I had the ones from Lummi Island. They are truly that unbelievable. Something about the mix of inland and Pacific waters, all the mountain rivers, the combination of salt and fresh water, and the way the tide goes in and out, against the islands, creates such a biodiversity of sea life and makes this one of the best places for shellfish. A freshly shucked platter of shellfish is almost always on the menu.

We get three different types of shrimp on Lummi. The small, light pink–striped shrimp taste so sweet and creamy that we usually serve them raw on their own or as ceviche. Blacktail shrimp are medium in size and darker in color, either brown and pink, and we like to cook them in hot rock salt. The biggest ones are bright red and translucent spot prawns, which we grill whole and brush with butter.

A platter of tiny pink singing scallops, served over ice, with a little fresh milk, shaved horseradish, and dill, is especially tasty during their short season when the bright roe is still attached. We serve this as often as possible.

In late winter, when the oysters are at their best, we serve them with pickles and the small, tart quince that also grows on the island. If the oysters are big, we like to grill them with brown butter, sage, lime juice, and tequila. They're delicious, especially on a crisp spring evening.

Clams are better cooked a little, at least with some acidity. Razor clam season is one of the most exciting times of year, because the local Indigenous people dig for them only when we have extremely low tides, usually during colder months, and then we sear them off on the plancha. Geoduck clams are available to us almost all year and we like to grill them. We also get small, purple clams that are extremely plump and sweet. Those we steam with green garlic and serve with our bread, which is made with wheat grown and milled just a few miles from The Willows.

During the winter, we get large honey mussels that are three to four inches big and are the creamiest, sweetest shellfish I've ever tasted.

BLUE CLAMS STEAMED WITH GREEN GARLIC
SERVES 4

INGREDIENTS

FOR THE GREEN GARLIC FERMENT

1 kg green garlic, cleaned and trimmed
25 g salt

FOR THE CLAMS

40 blue clams

FOR THE WILD ONION SAUCE

800 g wild onion tops
800 ml water

FOR THE GREEN GARLIC BUTTER

500 g green garlic tops
500 g unsalted butter

FOR THE GREEN GARLIC PURÉE

500 g green garlic bottoms

FOR THE GARNISH

40 green onion flowers
40 wild garlic mustard leaves

PREPARATION

FOR THE GREEN GARLIC FERMENT Coarsely chop the green garlic and massage with the salt. Tightly pack the green garlic in an earthenware crock and let sit at room temperature for 2 weeks. Wring the green garlic out in a cheesecloth, reserving the liquid and solids separately. Spread out the solids in a single layer in a dehydrator and dehydrate on low overnight. Once the solids are completely dry, remove and reserve for another use.

FOR THE CLAMS Soak the clams in fresh cold water overnight.

FOR THE WILD ONION SAUCE Blanch the wild onion tops then shock them in ice water. Wring out any excess water then blend the greens and the 800 ml of water in a blender on high speed until smooth. Pass through a fine strainer.

FOR THE GREEN GARLIC BUTTER Combine the green garlic tops with the butter and heat until the butter clarifies then strain.

FOR THE GREEN GARLIC PURÉE Toss the green garlic bottoms in oil and salt then wrap them in aluminum foil packets. Roast the packets directly on hot embers until tender. Carefully unwrap the green garlic bottoms then peel and discard the exterior layer and chop remaining garlic into a purée. Season the purée with salt and the green garlic ferment liquid, reserving 200 ml to cook clams, and set aside in piping bags.

TO COMPLETE

In a serving pot with a tight lid, heat 200 ml of the green garlic ferment liquid and the clams over medium heat. Cook until the clams just open then pipe the green garlic purée into each clam shell. Stir the wild onion sauce, green garlic butter, and any remaining green garlic purée into the broth and finish with the green onion flowers and wild garlic mustard leaves.

PINK SCALLOPS AND RADISH CREAM
SERVES 4

INGREDIENTS

1 kg pink singing scallops, live and in shells
2 black radishes
250 ml heavy cream

PREPARATION

Shuck the scallops and separate the adductor muscles and any roe. Reserve the roe and shells. Rinse the scallops in seawater and pat dry.

Peel and grate 250 g of the black radish and combine with the heavy cream. Infuse for 1 hour then strain, pressing on the solids.

TO COMPLETE

Arrange the scallop shells on a bed of ice and place 1 scallop and 1 piece of roe in each. Grate the remaining black radish and put a pinch on top of each scallop. Spoon the radish cream over each scallop and finish with salt.

VARIETY OF OYSTERS WITH ELDERBERRIES AND QUINCES

SERVES 4

INGREDIENTS

FOR THE PRESERVED QUINCES

2 quinces

FOR THE ELDERBERRY CAPERS

1 kg underripe elderberries

2 kg salt

500 ml apple cider vinegar

FOR THE CANTALOUPE MELON FERMENT

1 kg cantaloupe melon

25 g salt

FOR THE MIGNONETTE

100 g elderberry capers

100 g brunoised shallots

5 g crushed huacatay flowers

250 ml apple cider vinegar

250 ml cantaloupe melon ferment liquid (from above)

FOR THE OYSTERS

30 oysters of 6 different varieties

2 preserved quinces (from above)

PREPARATION

FOR THE PRESERVED QUINCES Let the quinces completely ripen on the bush. Seal the quinces in a vacuum bag and freeze for later use. Let the quinces thaw before using then cut in half and deseed.

FOR THE ELDERBERRY CAPERS Pick the elderberries off the stem and wash. Tightly pack them in a container with the salt then cover and refrigerate for 1 month. Rinse the elderberries then seal them in a vacuum bag with the apple cider vinegar and refrigerate for 1 month.

FOR THE CANTALOUPE MELON FERMENT Peel the cantaloupe melon and discard the seeds. Place the cantaloupe melon and salt in a food processor and coarsely chop. Seal the mixture in a vacuum bag and let ferment at room temperature for 14 days. Discard the melon and reserve the ferment liquid.

FOR THE MIGNONETTE Muddle the elderberry capers with a mortar and pestle until crushed then combine with the brunoised shallots and set aside. Muddle the huacatay flowers with the apple cider vinegar and cantaloupe melon ferment liquid then strain. Mix the shallot mixture with the strained liquid and season with salt.

TO COMPLETE

Shuck the oysters, reserving the top shells for presentation. Arrange the oysters in their shells on a bed of ice. Serve with ½ quince per person and 1 teaspoon of mignonette per oyster.

SEA URCHIN WITH RUTABAGA AND CHANTERELLES

SERVES 4

INGREDIENTS

FOR THE CHANTERELLE FERMENT

1 kg fresh chanterelle mushrooms

25 g salt

FOR THE RUTABAGA PURÉE

450 g rutabaga

50 ml grapeseed oil

50 ml heavy cream

4 sea urchins

50 ml chanterelle ferment liquid (from above)

5 fresh chanterelle mushrooms

50 ml olive oil

PREPARATION

FOR THE CHANTERELLE FERMENT Place the chanterelle mushrooms and salt in a food processor and coarsely chop. Seal the mixture in a vacuum bag and let sit at room temperature for 10 to 14 days. Discard the chanterelle mushrooms and reserve the ferment liquid.

FOR THE RUTABAGA PURÉE Cut the rutabaga into ⅔-inch (1.5 cm) slices. In a skillet over high heat, warm the grapeseed oil until hot. Char each slice of rutabaga until blackened. Seal the slices in a vacuum bag and cook at 212°F (100°C) for 1 hour. Blend the rutabaga with the heavy cream in a blender on high speed until smooth, and then pass through a fine-mesh strainer.

TO COMPLETE

Remove and clean the sea urchin tongues from the shell. Place a dime-sized amount of the rutabaga purée into each of 4 bowls. Arrange the urchin tongues around the purée and cover with 2 spoonfuls of the chanterelle ferment liquid. Cut the fresh chanterelle mushrooms into thin slices and place on top of the sea urchin then finish with a drizzle of olive oil.

SKEWERS

As the reigning champion of Lummi Island's official sport and favorite team day-off activity—beach fire grilling, sunset watching, and fire-works launching—I wanted to include some of my all-time favorite beach bites.

On our days off, we go to the beach, which is less than one hundred feet from the restaurant, make a huge fire, and spend a few hours grilling. Most of the time, we go fishing and make our lunch or dinner with our catch. I like to throw the largest oysters in the embers until they pop open or grill some fresh spot prawns still in the shell. Somehow, food always tastes better when cooked on the beach. It's also a reminder that what we do at the restaurant is something we enjoy doing even when the restaurant is closed.

These skewers are small dishes arranged to be grilled and then eaten in one bite. They change often and mostly feature vegetables from the garden, such as onions, summer squash, celtuce, or eggplant, basted with an oil made of herb seeds then grilled until golden brown and delicious, and served over a bed of herbs.

We also make bites of slowly cooked wild venison leg and tendon, brushed with a little chanterelle mushroom broth and studded with morel mushrooms that taste so good and help caramelize the meat. Octopus is grilled with chorizo and radicchio hearts and brushed with a sauce made from the head of the octopus, while geoduck clam is grilled whole then sliced and arranged on a skewer with slices of lardo and grilled again until crispy.

I wanted to extend that feeling of grilling on the beach to our menu so we added a section of BBQ bites for the spring and summer. It's fun to watch the reaction of our guests when they smell their skewers. It's a different and fun experience and perfect for summers by the beach.

GEODUCK CLAM SKEWERS

SERVES 4

INGREDIENTS

1 geoduck clam
110 ml heavy cream
100 g panko breadcrumbs
100 g lardo

PREPARATION

FOR THE GEODUCK Separate the geoduck liver from the body and syphon. Grill the body and syphon over hot charcoal until well charred then cut into ¾-inch-thick (2 cm) slices.

FOR THE LIVER SAUCE Roughly chop the geoduck liver and poach in the heavy cream until just cooked through. Blend the mixture in a blender on medium speed until thoroughly combined and hold warm.

FOR THE PANKO BREADCRUMBS Toast the panko breadcrumbs in a skillet with a spoonful of unsalted butter until golden.

FOR THE LARDO Cut the lardo into paper-thin slices.

TO COMPLETE

Skewer 3 slices of the geoduck body and syphon. Grill over very hot charcoal until charred then brush 1 side with the liver sauce and dip in the toasted panko breadcrumbs. Cover the other side of the geoduck with 1 slice of lardo and serve immediately. Repeat with the remaining geoduck, liver sauce, panko breadcrumbs, and lardo.

VENISON SKEWERS

SERVES 4

INGREDIENTS

1 venison leg
50 ml grapeseed oil
100 button mushrooms
40 fresh morel mushrooms
100 g salt
5 liters water

PREPARATION

FOR THE VENISON FAT Trim the venison, separating the large tendon from the fat cap. Finely chop the venison fat and sweat in the grapeseed oil until rendered. Strain off the rendered venison fat and reserve.

FOR THE VENISON Trim the venison leg into 1-inch (2.5 cm) cubes then brush with a small amount of the warm venison fat and let come to room temperature.

FOR THE MUSHROOM BOUILLON Steam the whole button mushrooms for 15 minutes or until cooked thoroughly then wring them out in cheesecloth, setting the liquid bouillon aside and reserving the button mushrooms for another use.

FOR THE MOREL MUSHROOMS In a skillet, sweat half of the morel mushrooms low and slow with a spoonful of venison fat and covered with a piece of parchment paper until tender, adding the mushroom bouillon a little at a time to glaze the mushrooms.

FOR THE VENISON TENDON Combine the salt and water and soak the venison tendon for 72 hours in this brine, refrigerated. Drain the tendon from the brine and seal in a vacuum bag. Cook at 175°F (80°C) for 72 hours then cut into 1-inch (2.5 cm) pieces.

TO COMPLETE

Skewer the venison leg, tendon, and morel mushrooms and heat gently on a grill over hot embers, being careful not to cook the venison beyond rare. Brush the skewers with some mushroom bouillon and hot, rendered venison fat and serve immediately. Repeat with the remaining venison leg, tendon, morel mushrooms, bouillon, and hot venison fat.

PORCINI MUSHROOM SKEWERS

SERVES 4

INGREDIENTS

FOR THE CHANTERELLE MUSHROOM FERMENT

1 kg fresh chanterelle
    mushrooms
25 g salt

FOR THE GREEN GARLIC FERMENT

1 kg green garlic, cleaned
    and trimmed
25 g salt

FOR THE WILDFLOWER SPICE MIX

200 g dehydrated,
    fermented green garlic
    (from above)
200 g dried wildflowers
50 g dried chive flowers

FOR THE WILDFLOWER SPICE SAUCE

250 g wildflower spice mix
500 g unsalted butter
200 ml fermented
    chanterelle mushroom
    liquid (from above)
50 ml fermented green
    garlic liquid (from
    above)
20 ml apple cider vinegar

FOR THE SKEWERS

5 fresh porcini
    mushrooms
10 young shallots

PREPARATION

FOR THE CHANTERELLE MUSHROOM FERMENT **Coarsely** chop the chanterelle mushrooms and massage with the salt. Tightly pack the mushrooms into an earthenware crock and let sit at room temperature for 2 weeks. Wring out the mushrooms in a cheesecloth, reserving the liquid and solids separately. Spread out the solids in a single layer in a dehydrator and dehydrate on low overnight. Once the solids are completely dry, remove and reserve for another use.

FOR THE GREEN GARLIC FERMENT **Coarsely chop the** green garlic and massage with the salt. Tightly pack the garlic into an earthenware crock and let sit at room temperature for 2 weeks. Wring out the green garlic in a cheesecloth, reserving the liquid and solids separately. Spread out the solids in a single layer in a dehydrator and dehydrate on low overnight. Once the solids are completely dry, remove from the dehydrator and set aside.

FOR THE WILDFLOWER SPICE MIX **Blend the dry** fermented green garlic, dried wildflowers, and dried chive flowers in a blender on high speed until it forms a fine powder then sift through a fine strainer.

FOR THE WILDFLOWER SPICE SAUCE **Toast the wildflower** spice mix in 100 g of foaming butter over high heat then deglaze with some of the fermented chanterelle mushroom and green garlic liquids. Season with apple cider vinegar and salt.

FOR THE SKEWERS Separate the porcini mushroom caps from the stems. Slice half of the caps into very thin slices and marinate in a little of the chanterelle mushroom ferment liquid and grapeseed oil. Cut the remaining porcini mushroom caps and stems into thick slices and coat with the wildflower spice sauce.

Peel the shallots and toss them in grapeseed oil and a pinch of salt. Wrap in an aluminum foil packet and bury in hot embers to cook for 10 minutes then allow to cool completely.

TO COMPLETE

Skewer a piece of the porcini cap, the porcini stem, a shallot, and several slices of the marinated porcini caps. Grill over high heat until the mushrooms are nicely charred and cooked through and serve immediately. Repeat with the remaining porcini caps, porcini stems, shallots, and marinated porcini caps.

OCTOPUS SKEWERS

SERVES 4

INGREDIENTS

1 (4 kg) octopus
100 ml grapeseed oil
2 heads radicchio
20 slices hard chorizo

PREPARATION

FOR THE OCTOPUS Boil the octopus for 30 minutes then let cool. Remove the octopus from the water and dry with a fan. Separate the tentacles from the head and cut the tentacles into thick slices.

FOR THE OCTOPUS GLAZE Slice the octopus head into thin strips and sauté in 50 ml grapeseed oil over medium heat until caramelized. Place the strips in a bowl, cover with aluminum foil, and let cool. Once cool, strain off any liquid that accumulates and set aside. Reserve the octopus strips for another use.

FOR THE RADICCHIO Cut the radicchio into quarters and sauté in 50 ml grapeseed oil over high heat until charred and cooked through then let cool. Cut the charred radicchio into thick slices.

TO COMPLETE

Skewer a slice of the octopus tentacles, a piece of the radicchio, and a slice of chorizo and brush with the octopus glaze. Grill, basting with more of the octopus glaze, over hot embers until well caramelized and serve immediately. Repeat with the remaining octopus tentacles, radicchio, chorizo, and octopus glaze.

Forest covers most of Lummi Island and just a small area has a few roads, a few homes, and a single store that carries only the essentials you need to survive a few days on the island. Of course, the closest gas station is ten miles away—on the mainland. Parts of the island almost give the impression that they have never been seen by human eyes.

All this makes Lummi one of the best places to forage for wild foods, and with the almost nonstop rain, one of the best places to collect wild mushrooms, too. There are too many types of mushrooms to count and there are times when the island is literally carpeted with wild mushrooms. Even though they look completely different, the flavors can be so subtle that we serve three different wild mushroom stews, side by side, to highlight the unique tastes and textures of each variety.

While mushrooms grow on the island almost all year long, the forests are otherwise bare throughout winter and the first sign of spring is the spears of swamp cabbage shooting up through the forest floor, with large green leaves and yellow flowers that scent the whole island. The cabbage grows in the swamp and every morning in spring, the chefs tromp around in the mud, collecting the spears on their way to work. The leaves look like banana leaves but have a flavor like the herb lovage, so they are perfect for wrapping and steaming pieces of whitefish or tender vegetables.

The first spring plants growing on the island or from the farm are so tender it only takes a few seconds with very light steam to cook them. It's important to dress the ingredients just before they are steamed, and to serve them immediately and with no accompaniments. I love to share the natural flavors of spring in this way, as it focuses the palate on the flavors and textures of the meal to come.

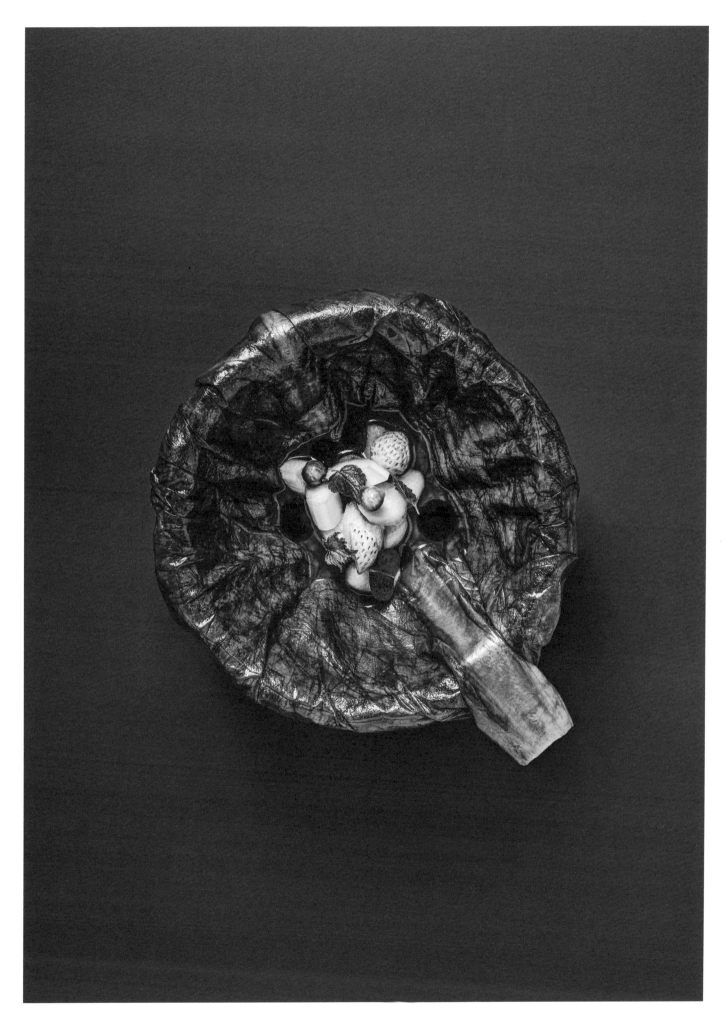

STEAMED ITEMS

BLACK COD STEAMED WITH
BLACK CURRANTS

SERVES 4

INGREDIENTS

3 kg yogurt
4 cod fillets
35 g salt
500 ml water
5 black currant branches
20 black currant berries
4 skunk cabbage leaves
270 ml grapeseed oil
270 ml parsley oil (see page 43)

PREPARATION

Hang the yogurt in cheesecloth set over a bowl and store overnight in the refrigerator. Collect the whey and reserve the strained yogurt for another use.

Prepare each cod fillet, leaving the skin on and the pin bones in. Dissolve the salt in the water and brine them for 30 minutes then pat dry. Cut them into 4 roughly 50 g portions.

Pick any small tender leaves from the currant branches and set aside for garnish. Leave larger leaves on the branches. Remove the currant berries from the stems and set aside.

Blanch the skunk cabbage leaves in boiling water for 2 minutes then shock them in ice water. Remove and pat dry.

Chop the black currant branches and blend the wood with the grapeseed oil and parsley oil in a blender on high speed for 10 minutes or until smooth. Cool then strain through a cheesecloth.

TO COMPLETE

Spray the skunk cabbage leaves with nonstick spray and place 1 portion of cod, 3 currant leaves, 4 currant berries, and 50 g of yogurt whey in each leaf. Wrap into packets, place on a baking sheet and warm at 325°F (160°C) for 6 minutes. Open the skunk cabbage leaves into bowls and finish with a spoonful of the black currant wood oil and a pinch of fresh currant leaves.

GREEN STRAWBERRIES STEAMED WITH
RHUBARB AND GOOSEBERRIES

SERVES 4

INGREDIENTS

FOR THE WHEY

3 kg yogurt

FOR THE SKUNK CABBAGE

4 skunk cabbage leaves

FOR THE BLACK CURRANT WOOD OIL

400 g black currant wood, chopped
100 ml grapeseed oil
100 ml parsley oil (see page 43)

FOR ASSEMBLY

24 green strawberries
12 gooseberries
2 stalks green rhubarb, sliced
12 black currant leaves
16 black currant berries
20 oxalis leaves
250 ml whey (from above)

PREPARATION

FOR THE WHEY Hang the yogurt in cheesecloth set over a bowl and store overnight in the refrigerator. Collect the whey and reserve the strained yogurt for another use.

FOR THE SKUNK CABBAGE Blanch the skunk cabbage leaves in boiling water for 2 minutes then shock them in ice water. Remove and pat dry.

FOR THE BLACK CURRANT WOOD OIL Blend the chopped black currant wood, grapeseed oil, and parsley oil in a blender on high speed for 10 minutes or until smooth. Cool then strain through a cheesecloth.

TO COMPLETE

Place 6 green strawberries, 3 gooseberries, 3 slices rhubarb, 3 currant leaves, 4 currant berries, 3 oxalis leaves, and about 60 ml whey in each skunk cabbage leaf. Wrap into packets and secure with skewers. Warm in a 325°F (160°C) oven for 6 minutes. Open the skunk cabbage leaves into bowls and finish with a spoonful of black currant wood oil and a pinch of oxalis leaves.

A STEW OF CHANTERELLE MUSHROOMS

SERVES 4

INGREDIENTS

2 kg fresh chanterelle mushrooms
1 kg button mushrooms
250 g unsalted butter

PREPARATION

FOR THE CHANTERELLE MUSHROOMS Cut the stems from the chanterelle mushroom caps. Reserve the stems for making the stock and butter. Reserve the small, firm caps for slicing and tear the larger caps into rustic pieces.

FOR THE MUSHROOM STOCK Steam the button mushrooms for 10 minutes then let cool. Wring out the mushrooms in cheesecloth, reserving the liquid. In a saucepan over medium heat, bring the liquid to a boil, add all the chanterelle mushroom stems, remove from heat, and let steep for 10 minutes and strain, reserving the stock and stems separately.

FOR THE MUSHROOM BUTTER Measure 250 g of the chanterelle mushroom stems and combine with the butter and cook in a pot on the stovetop at 175°F (80°C) for 2 hours or until the butter clarifies. Strain, reserving the butter.

TO COMPLETE

Stew the torn chanterelle mushroom pieces with a tiny amount of the mushroom stock and mushroom butter until tender. Thinly slice some of the small, raw chanterelle mushroom caps and arrange around the inside of each of 4 bowls. Add a spoonful of the cooked chanterelle mushrooms and coat with some of the hot mushroom stock and a drizzle of the mushroom butter.

A STEW OF PORCINI MUSHROOMS

SERVES 4

INGREDIENTS

2 kg fresh porcini mushrooms
1 kg button mushrooms
250 g unsalted butter

PREPARATION

FOR THE PORCINI MUSHROOMS Cut the stems from the porcini mushroom caps. Reserve the stems for making the stock and butter. Reserve the small, firm caps for slicing and tear the larger caps into rustic pieces.

FOR THE MUSHROOM STOCK Steam the button mushrooms for 10 minutes then let cool. Wring out the mushrooms in a cheesecloth, reserving the liquid. In a saucepan over medium heat, bring the liquid to a boil, add all the porcini mushroom stems, remove from heat, and let steep for 10 minutes. Strain, reserving the stock and stems separately.

FOR THE MUSHROOM BUTTER Measure 250 g of the porcini mushroom stems and combine with the butter and cook in a pot on the stovetop at 175°F (80°C) for 2 hours or until the butter clarifies. Strain, reserving the butter.

TO COMPLETE

Stew the torn porcini mushroom pieces with a tiny amount of the mushroom stock and mushroom butter until tender. Thinly slice some of the small, raw porcini mushroom caps and arrange around the inside of each of 4 bowls. Add a spoonful of the cooked porcini mushrooms and coat with some of the hot mushroom stock and a drizzle of the mushroom butter.

A STEW OF MATSUTAKE MUSHROOMS
SERVES 4

INGREDIENTS

2 kg fresh matsutake mushrooms
1 kg button mushrooms
250 g unsalted butter

PREPARATION

FOR THE MATSUTAKE MUSHROOMS Cut the stems from
the matsutake mushroom caps. Reserve the stems
for making the stock and butter. Reserve the small, firm
caps for slicing and tear the larger caps into rustic
pieces.

FOR THE MUSHROOM STOCK Steam the button
mushrooms for 10 minutes then let cool. Wring out the
mushrooms in a cheesecloth, reserving the liquid.
In a saucepan over medium heat, bring the liquid to a
boil, add all the matsutake mushroom stems, remove
from heat, and let steep for 10 minutes. Strain, reserving
the stock and stems separately.

FOR THE MUSHROOM BUTTER Measure 250 g of the
matsutake mushroom stems and combine with the
butter and cook in a pot on the stovetop at 175°F (80°C)
for 2 hours or until the butter clarifies. Strain, reserving
the butter.

TO COMPLETE

Stew the torn matsutake mushroom pieces with a tiny
amount of the mushroom stock and mushroom butter
until tender. Thinly slice some of the small, raw
matsutake mushroom caps and arrange around the
inside of each of 4 bowls. Add a spoonful of the cooked
matsutake mushrooms and coat with some of the hot
mushroom stock and a drizzle of the mushroom butter.

A STEW OF YELLOWFOOT MUSHROOMS
SERVES 4

INGREDIENTS

2 kg fresh yellowfoot mushrooms
1 kg button mushrooms
250 g unsalted butter

PREPARATION

FOR THE YELLOWFOOT MUSHROOMS Cut the stems from
the yellowfoot mushroom caps. Reserve the stems
for making the stock and butter. Reserve the small, firm
caps for slicing and tear the larger caps into rustic
pieces.

FOR THE MUSHROOM STOCK Steam the button
mushrooms for 10 minutes then let cool. Wring out the
mushrooms in a cheesecloth, reserving the liquid.
In a saucepan over medium heat, bring the liquid to a
boil, add all the yellowfoot mushroom stems, remove
from heat, and let steep for 10 minutes. Strain, reserving
the stock and stems separately.

FOR THE MUSHROOM BUTTER Measure 250 g of the
yellowfoot mushroom stems and combine with the
butter and cook in a pot on the stovetop at 175°F (80°C)
for 2 hours or until the butter clarifies. Strain, reserving
the butter.

TO COMPLETE

Stew the torn yellowfoot mushroom pieces with a tiny
amount of the mushroom stock and mushroom butter
until tender. Thinly slice some of the small, raw
yellowfoot mushroom caps and arrange around the
inside of each of 4 bowls. Add a spoonful of the cooked
yellowfoot mushrooms and coat with some of the hot
mushroom stock and a drizzle of the mushroom butter.

CRAB HEAD AND BREAD TO DIP IN IT

SERVES 4

INGREDIENTS

FOR THE CRAB
10 liters seawater
4 Dungeness crabs

FOR THE DUNGENESS CRAB STOCK
2 kg mussels
2 Dungeness crab shells
    (from above)
Liquid reserved from
    4 Dungeness crab heads
    (from above)

FOR THE CRAB BUTTER
500 g unsalted butter,
    at room temperature
250 to 350 ml strong crab
    stock

FOR THE CRAB CREAM
2 Dungeness crab shells
    (from above)
3.75 liters heavy cream

FOR THE CRAB CUSTARD
320 g farm fresh egg yolks
60 g crab butter, melted
    (from above)
300 g crab cream (from
    above)
240 g Dungeness crab
    stock (from above)
20 g salt

1 loaf rustic bread

PREPARATION

FOR THE CRAB Bring the seawater to a boil then pour over the Dungeness crabs and poach for 23 minutes. Remove the crabs from the seawater then strain the crab head liquid and chill it. Clean the crab meat from the shells, reserving both and putting the cleaned crab heads aside for serving.

FOR THE DUNGENESS CRAB STOCK Steam the mussels, then strain and reserve the mussel stock. Smash 2 of the reserved crab shells with a large pestle and pack tightly in a pot. Cover with the mussel stock and the crab head liquid and boil for 45 minutes. Strain and chill immediately.

FOR THE CRAB BUTTER Combine the room-temperature butter and the strong crab stock and mix until smooth.

FOR THE CRAB CREAM Smash the 2 remaining crab shells with a large pestle and pack tightly into a pot. Cover with the heavy cream and boil until reduced by half then strain and chill the cream.

FOR THE CRAB CUSTARD Blend all of the ingredients with an immersion blender until smooth. Transfer to a medium metal bowl and place over a pan of simmering water. Slowly cook, whisking continuously, until a custard forms.

TO COMPLETE

Toast the rustic bread in the oven and cut into thick slices. Warm the crab meat and crab custard separately in small pots. Spoon some of the warm custard and warm crab meat into a warmed crab head shell. Cover with the crab butter and Dungeness crab stock and serve with the toasted bread.

SMOKEHOUSE & GRILL

A whiff of smoke from our smokehouse and grill is usually the first sign that you have arrived at The Willows Inn. At some point, almost everyone ends up crowding around to see what's cooking and to sneak a taste. It has got to be one of the best stations in the kitchen, as you're working outside in the garden, looking out into the sunset and the ocean every night. It's certainly the most exciting and beautiful grill station I've ever seen.

Being assigned to the grill and smokehouse is a coveted position, but it has one of the earliest starts, with the daily chore of splitting and stacking tall piles of wood and firing up the smokehouse first thing.

This is a special type of cooking. The smokehouse needs to be tended for hours but requires very little attention. The nuances of wood and weather are mastered only with regular practice but can transform fresh seafood unlike any other cooking method. The best flavor comes from a long, light smoke, with the smoke not in a thick cloud but just wafting over the food.

I have smoked with different types of wood and it is amazing how distinct their flavors are, but we only use green alder wood for our smokehouse. It's green because it is freshly cut from the tree and still "green" rather than dry or stripped of its bark. This is important, because wet wood smolders and doesn't catch fire and the flavor of the food is softer, sweeter, and more delicate than food cooked with dry wood, which can be bitter, oversmoked, and very strong.

The grill is the opposite, as the wood needs to be extremely dry hardwood. We use maple mostly and sometimes birch to fuel the wood-fired grill, but for many recipes, we add an aromatic layer just before cooking, which enhances the flavor and seasoning tremendously, and greatly expands the capabilities of the grill. Dried oregano stems are layered over the hot embers before grilling bundles of runner beans, while a branch from the flowering bay tree infuses halibut with such a distinct flavor and a juniper branch perfumes grilled wild venison.

Some of the recipes in this chapter—like the Smoked Black Cod Doughnuts or Smoked Sockeye Salmon—call for a long, cold smoke, which is a method in which the smoking is done at a low temperature and flavors, more than cooks, the ingredient. Whereas the items being grilled are best with very little smoke at high temperature. Either way, cooking over wood adds a ton of flavor.

SMOKED MUSSELS

SERVES 4

INGREDIENTS

200 ml white wine
40 mussels

PREPARATION

FOR THE MUSSELS Bring the white wine to a boil, add the mussels, cover, and steam for 1 minute or until just opened then shock them in ice water. Shuck the mussels, reserving the shells, and lay them out on a tray over ice. Put the tray of mussels in the lower rack of a smoker for 3 hours. Remove from the smoker, reserving any smoked mussel juices separately.

FOR THE MUSSEL SAUCE In a saucepan, bring a thin layer of grapeseed oil to a smoke point and sear 10 of the smoked mussels, turning, until caramelized on both sides. Deglaze the pan with the excess smoked mussel juices and reduce until slightly thicker. Pour the mussels and juices into a container, wrap tightly with plastic wrap, and let infuse at room temperature for 1 hour then strain and reserve the sauce.

TO COMPLETE

In a sauté pan, bring a thin layer of grapeseed oil to a smoke point and sear 10 of the smoked mussels, turning, until caramelized on both sides. Return the mussels to their shells, brush with the mussel sauce, and serve immediately. Repeat with the remaining mussels.

SMOKED TUNA WITH CUCUMBER SEEDS AND HORSERADISH

SERVES 4

INGREDIENTS

200 g salt
1 liter water
1 albacore tuna loin
1 kg cucumbers
50 g fresh parsley seeds
50 g fresh dill seeds
10 g fresh fennel seeds
100 ml lemon juice
1 (25 g) piece fresh horseradish, peeled

PREPARATION

Combine the salt and water to make a salt brine and brine the albacore tuna loin for 20 minutes then drain. Smoke the albacore tuna loin over green alder wood for 1 hour.

Cut the cucumbers in half and remove and reserve the seeds, saving the flesh for another use. Using a mortar and pestle, grind the fresh parsley, dill, and fennel seeds with enough salt and lemon juice to make a paste. Grate the horseradish.

TO COMPLETE

Cut the albacore tuna loin into chunks and toss with the cucumber seeds, seed paste, and grated horseradish. Serve cold in chilled bowls.

CURED ROCKFISH WITH GRILLED KELP

SERVES 4

INGREDIENTS

4 whole red rockfish
200 ml white wine
5 kg mussels
2 dried shitake mushrooms
2 smoked and dried smelts
1 ½ sheets gelatin
100 g kelp
100 ml grapeseed oil

PREPARATION

FOR THE ROCKFISH Scale the rockfish completely and set aside the 2 fillets with the skin attached. Reserve all the bones. In a shallow cake pan, completely cover the fillets with a heavy coating of kosher salt. Cure in the fridge for 24 hours, then rinse and pat dry the fillets. Quickly grill the skin side only over hot embers until the skin is charred but the meat still raw, then thinly slice.

FOR THE MUSSEL STOCK Simmer the white wine and mussels for 10 minutes or until they just open then strain, reserving the liquid.

FOR THE ROCKFISH STOCK Grill the reserved rockfish bones over hot embers until well charred. Combine all but 1 of the bones with the dried shiitake mushrooms, dried smelts, and the mussel stock in a pot. Warm over medium heat, avoiding a boil, for 1 hour then strain and chill the stock.

FOR THE ROCKFISH GEL Combine 500 ml of the rockfish stock with the gelatin sheets and refrigerate.

FOR THE KELP OIL Grill the kelp over hot embers until charred then spread in a single layer in a dehydrator and dehydrate on low for 24 hours. Seal the reserved grilled rockfish bone and the grapeseed oil in a vacuum bag and cook at 140°F (60°C) for 4 hours then strain. Blend the rockfish bone oil with the dehydrated kelp in a blender on high speed then let sit overnight in the refrigerator then strain.

TO COMPLETE

Lay 3 slices of the cured rockfish in each of 4 chilled bowls and cover with some of the chilled remaining rockfish stock. Add rockfish gel around the slices and finish with the kelp oil.

BLACK COD COLLARS GRILLED WITH MISO

SERVES 4

INGREDIENTS

FOR THE MISO
500 g pine nuts
200 ml hot water
500 g rice koji
100 g salt

FOR THE BLACK COD COLLARS
3 black cod collars
35 g salt
500 ml water

PREPARATION

FOR THE MISO Quickly submerge the pine nuts in the hot water until soft. Drain and then put the pine nuts, along with the rice koji and salt, into a food processor and purée. Adjust with water to make a thick paste. Place in a jar to ferment for 2 months in a dark room.

FOR THE BLACK COD COLLARS Split the collars in half and clean them of excess skin. Dissolve the salt in the water and brine the collars for 20 minutes then rinse and pat dry.

TO COMPLETE

Evenly coat the black cod collars with the miso. Grill until cooked and well blackened, then separate the meat and skin from the bones and fins and arrange on 4 plates.

SMOKED BLACK COD DOUGHNUTS
SERVES 4

INGREDIENTS

950 ml whole milk
260 ml egg yolk
400 g yeast
2 kg all-purpose flour
200 g sugar
100 g kosher salt
1 (500 g) whole black cod
35 g salt
500 ml water
5 g dried, ground seaweed

PREPARATION

FOR THE DOUGH Using a stand mixer with a paddle
attachment, mix the milk, egg yolks, and yeast until
foamy. Add the flour, sugar, and salt and mix on low
speed for 5 minutes. Transfer the dough to a large bowl,
cover, and proof at room temperature for 1 to 2 hours or
until doubled in size.

On a floured work surface, roll the dough until about
½-inch (1 cm) thick then cut into 20 g portions. The
dough can be used immediately or frozen.

FOR THE DOUGHNUTS Cut the black cod lengthwise
down the center and fillet. Dissolve the salt in the water
and brine the cod for 30 minutes. Drain the fillets and let
dry, covered, overnight in the refrigerator. Cold smoke
the fillets for 6 hours then cut into 1-inch (2.5 cm) cubes.
Wrap the small cubes of black cod in the pieces of
dough, sealing the bottoms well.

TO COMPLETE

Let the doughnuts proof for 30 minutes on a floured
pan then fry at 325°F (160°C) until golden brown on all
sides. Finish the doughnuts with a dusting of the dried,
ground seaweed.

SMOKED SOCKEYE SALMON
SERVES 4

INGREDIENTS

6 liters water
2.5 kg ice
1.8 kg salt
4 Lummi Island wild sockeye
    salmon fillets, skin on
200 g brown sugar
200 g unsalted butter
50 ml verjus

PREPARATION

FOR THE SALMON Combine the water, ice, and salt to
make a 20% brine. Cut each salmon fillet into 4 portions
and brine for 32 minutes then rinse in a bath of fresh
water and pat dry. Lay the salmon on parchment paper,
wrap it tightly, and refrigerate overnight. Smoke the
salmon for about 4 hours.

FOR THE GLAZE Melt the brown sugar and butter in
a small saucepan over medium-low heat until the sugar
has just melted and incorporated into the butter then
blend with an immersion blender until the texture is
creamy. Season with verjus and salt.

TO COMPLETE

Use an offset spatula to remove the skin from the
smoked salmon fillets. Warm the salmon in a 200°F
(93°C) oven for 4 to 6 minutes then brush with the
salmon glaze and serve.

Hearty vegetable cooking is at the core of our menu. There are times when the kitchen gets absolutely crushed with so many beautiful vegetables from the farm that just finding a place to stand in the kitchen is a struggle. The farm brings more and more every day and it always makes me smile when I pull a bin of vegetables from the walk-in refrigerator, expecting them to be cold, and discover they are still warm from the sun and smell like the farm's soil.

It can be so much more difficult to know how to treat a vegetable than it is to cook a steak, and the cooking must be much more nuanced. Flavors need to be coaxed from vegetables and accented with just the right seasoning; the carving and cooking is so important. It takes the whole team to create these recipes and nothing makes us happier than seeing the joy on someone's face after taking a bite of one of our vegetable dishes.

Vegetables are like precious jewels in our kitchen. We are at the farm every day throughout all the seasons, and watch every single vegetable grow from a tiny seed. So, in the summer, when we are standing in the kitchen, holding a large summer squash that is just picked and fragrant, and still warm to the touch, the feeling is magical.

Over time, the main benefit of having our own farm has been the ability to grow varieties that are not otherwise available. We work to find the exact right variety as well as just how to cook it. But the other, more obvious benefit is freshness, which, for me, comes across in fragrance. The strong fragrance of fresh vegetables is so fleeting and dissipates in just a few days or even a few hours in some cases. Capturing the full flavor and aroma is what makes these recipes the most satisfying to cook and eat. Hearty vegetable cooking is truly my passion.

TOASTED KALE CHIPS

SERVES 4

INGREDIENTS

FOR THE TRUFFLE
EMULSION

300 g chicken glace

120 g squid ink

240 ml button mushroom
stock (see page 101)

70 ml apple cider vinegar

200 ml truffle oil

FOR THE RYE CRISPS

240 g rye bread

500 g unsalted butter

FOR THE KALE CHIPS

30 large, unblemished
Lacinato kale leaves

PREPARATION

FOR THE TRUFFLE EMULSION Blend the chicken glace, squid ink, button mushroom stock, and apple cider vinegar in a blender on high speed until completely incorporated. Reduce the speed to low and slowly drizzle in the truffle oil until stiff peaks form. Season with additional apple cider vinegar and salt and put into a piping bag.

FOR THE RYE CRISPS Cut the rye bread into small dime-sized pieces and process in a food processor to create fine crumbs. In a 350°F (176°C) oven, toast the rye crumbs in the butter until golden brown. Drain the crumbs and set on paper towels.

FOR THE KALE CHIPS Remove the kale leaves from the stalk. Arrange the leaves evenly on a baking sheet lined with a nonstick silicone mat and sprayed with a thin coat of nonstick spray. Use nonstick metal bars to allow for a wave shape. Roast at 325°F (160°C), rotating the baking sheet every 5 minutes, until the veins of the kale turn golden brown. Season lightly with salt and arrange in single layers to avoid breakage in airtight containers.

TO COMPLETE

Dot each toasted kale leaf with the truffle emulsion and sprinkle each dot with the toasted rye crumbs.

ONIONS FILLED WITH CHEESE

SERVES 4

INGREDIENTS

FOR THE ONIONS

5 small spring onions

FOR THE ONION SAUCE

500 g cipollini onions,
thinly sliced

30 g unsalted butter

FOR SERVING

200 g fromage blanc

25 marjoram leaves

PREPARATION

FOR THE ONIONS Halve and peel the spring onions. Char the flat side of the spring onions in a skillet over high heat until black. Seal in a vacuum bag and cook at 175°F (80°C) for 15 minutes or until tender. Carefully peel the onion layers, keeping the charred petals intact.

FOR THE ONION SAUCE In a skillet, sweat the cipollini onions in the butter over medium heat until very soft. Strain the mixture, season the juices with salt, and reserve the solids for another use.

TO COMPLETE

In a 350°F (176°C) oven, heat the spring onion petals until warm. Place a small dollop of the fromage blanc inside each spring onion petal and arrange, wrapping petal around and placing cut-side down, in 4 bowls. Warm the onion sauce and add a spoonful to the bottom of each bowl then garnish each spring onion with a marjoram leaf.

ONIONS FILLED WITH DRIED SHELLFISH
SERVES 4

INGREDIENTS

FOR THE GREEN GARLIC FERMENT
500 g green garlic tops (no bulbs)
25 g salt

FOR THE ONIONS
5 small spring onions

FOR THE DRIED SHELLFISH SAUCE
200 g dried mixed shellfish
20 g dehydrated fermented green garlic (from above)
540 ml grapeseed oil
20 g diced shallots
50 ml fermented green garlic liquid (from above)

FOR SERVING
25 marjoram leaves

PREPARATION

FOR THE GREEN GARLIC FERMENT Coarsely chop the green garlic tops and massage with the salt. Tightly pack the green garlic in an earthenware crock and let sit at room temperature for 2 weeks. Wring out the green garlic in a cheesecloth, reserving the liquid and solids separately. Spread out the solids in a single layer in a dehydrator and dehydrate on low overnight. Once the solids are completely dry, remove from the dehydrator.

FOR THE ONIONS Halve and peel the spring onions. Char the flat side of the spring onions in a skillet over high heat until black. Seal in a vacuum bag and cook at 175°F (80°C) for 15 minutes or until tender. Carefully peel the onion layers, keeping the charred petals intact.

FOR THE DRIED SHELLFISH SAUCE Separately hydrate the dried mixed shellfish and dehydrated fermented green garlic in hot water for 1 hour. Strain both, reserving the liquid and solids separately. Finely chop the shellfish.

Heat the grapeseed oil to 330°F (165°C) and fry the shellfish and shallots until dark brown in color then strain, reserving the oil. Blend the fried shellfish and shallots with the hydrated green garlic in a blender on low speed then emulsify with some of the reserved frying oil and some of the reserved hydrating liquid until the texture is chunky and creamy. Season with salt and the green garlic ferment liquid.

TO COMPLETE

In a 350°F (176°C) oven, heat the spring onion petals until warm. Place a small dollop of the dried shellfish sauce inside each spring onion petal and arrange, wrapping petal around and placing cut-side down, in 4 bowls. Warm the shellfish sauce and add a spoonful to the bottom of each bowl, along with a spoonful of the frying oil then garnish each spring onion with a marjoram leaf.

FALL SQUASH AND FERMENTED SEEDS
SERVES 4

INGREDIENTS

FOR THE PUMPKIN SEED MISO
500 g pumpkin seeds
500 g rice koji
100 g salt

FOR THE SQUASH
4 hard fall squash; possible varieties include Cinderella, sugar pie pumpkin, kabocha or Hubbard squash
8 dried dill crowns

FOR THE DILL BUTTER
500 g unsalted butter, at room temperature
100 g dried dill seeds

FOR THE SQUASH SEEDS
500 g reserved squash seeds

FOR THE DILL SALT
20 g dried dill seeds
20 g sea salt

PREPARATION

FOR THE PUMPKIN SEED MISO Toast the pumpkin seeds in a 325°F (160°C) oven until golden brown then hydrate the seeds in simmering water until just soft. While still warm, drain the seeds and mash them with the rice koji and salt. Pack into a sterile, airtight container and let ferment in a warm, dark place for 3 months.

FOR THE SQUASH Carve the squash into crescent shapes then clean out and reserve the seeds and brush each piece of squash with grapeseed oil. Line 4 half baking sheets with parchment paper, arrange 2 dill crowns on each, and lay the cut squash on top. Pour 200 ml of water into the bottom of each baking sheet, cover, and roast in a 325°F (160°C) oven, rotating the baking sheets every 20 minutes, for 1 hour or until the squash is cooked and completely tender throughout.

FOR THE DILL BUTTER Crush the dill seeds into the butter using a mortar and pestle.

FOR THE SQUASH SEEDS Boil the reserved squash seeds for 1 hour and drain. Gently peel off and discard the exterior layer of the seeds and reserve the soft interior flesh.

FOR THE DILL SALT Toast the dill seeds then lightly grind in a mortar and pestle and combine with the sea salt.

TO COMPLETE

Brush the squash pieces with the dill butter and warm, uncovered, in a 350°F (175°C) oven. Warm the pumpkin seed miso in a small saucepan. Carve the skin off the squash and cut each into 4 equal portions. Finish with a small dollop of the pumpkin seed miso, then sprinkle on a few squash seeds and a pinch of the dill salt.

SUMMER SQUASH AND NASTURTIUM FLOWERS

SERVES 4

INGREDIENTS

FOR THE LOVAGE SALT
50 g fresh lovage leaves
50 g salt

FOR THE LOVAGE OIL
200 ml grapeseed oil
200 g fresh lovage leaves

FOR THE SQUASH
4 large heirloom summer
  squash
20 sprigs fresh chamomile

FOR THE NASTURTIUM PURÉE
250 g fresh nasturtium
  flowers
270 ml grapeseed oil
10 ml apple cider vinegar
10 ml verjus
10 g Dijon mustard

FOR THE CHAMOMILE BUTTER
100 g dried chamomile
  flowers
500 g unsalted butter,
  at room temperature

FOR THE SQUASH BLOSSOMS
4 small spring onions
8 squash blossoms
5 daylilies
100 g fromage blanc
20 ml verjus

FOR THE GARNISH
24 fresh nasturtium
  flowers
6 sprigs fresh chamomile

PREPARATION

FOR THE LOVAGE SALT Blend the fresh lovage leaves and salt in a blender then lay out in a thin layer on a sheet tray and dry in a warm place for 2 days. Once dried, blend again to make a fine salt.

FOR THE LOVAGE OIL Blend the grapeseed oil and lovage leaves in a blender on high speed for 15 minutes. Infuse overnight in the refrigerator and then strain.

FOR THE SQUASH Cut the squash in half then brush with grapeseed oil and season with salt. Line 4 half baking sheets with parchment paper, arrange chamomile sprigs on each, and lay the cut squash on top. Pour 200 ml of water into the bottom of each baking sheet, cover, and roast in a 325°F (160°C) oven, rotating the baking sheets every 20 minutes, for 40 minutes or until the squash is cooked and completely tender throughout.

FOR THE NASTURTIUM PURÉE Blend the nasturtium flowers, grapeseed oil, apple cider vinegar, verjus, and Dijon mustard in a blender on high speed until smooth then pour through a fine-mesh strainer.

FOR THE CHAMOMILE BUTTER Crush the dried chamomile flowers into the butter using a mortar and pestle.

FOR THE SQUASH BLOSSOMS Halve the onions and steam until very soft and tender. Remove the petals from 4 of the squash blossoms and all of the daylilies. Roughly chop both petals with the steamed onions. Mix with the fromage blanc and season with verjus and salt. Fill the remaining 4 fresh squash blossoms halfway with the onion and fromage blanc mixture.

TO COMPLETE

Place a large spoonful of the nasturtium purée and a small spoonful of the lovage oil into each of 4 small bowls and arrange the nasturtium petals to replicate flowers. Steam the squash blossoms in a steamer basket over boiling water for 1 minute and brush with olive oil. Brush the squash with the chamomile butter and then warm, uncovered, in a 350°F (175°C) oven until heated through.

Dust the roasted squash with the lovage salt and small sprigs of fresh chamomile. Place alongside the steamed squash blossoms and the nasturtium sauce, then serve.

HEIRLOOM PEAS AND BITTER GREENS

SERVES 4

INGREDIENTS

100 g Rioja peas
350 g sunchokes
1 dried smelt
100 ml grapeseed oil
3 heads radicchio
40 g caviar
10 ml olive oil

PREPARATION

FOR THE PEAS Soak the Rioja peas in cold water overnight. Rinse then cover with fresh cold water in a large stockpot. Add 50 g of the sunchokes, bring to a simmer, and let cook for 4 to 6 hours. Strain off and reserve the liquid. Discard the sunchokes and cool the peas at room temperature. Add the dried smelt to the pea cooking liquid and steep for 1 hour then strain, discarding the smelt and reserving the stock.

FOR THE SUNCHOKE PURÉE Cut the remaining 300 g of sunchokes in half and arrange, cut-side down, on a baking sheet. Pour 100 ml of water and the grapeseed oil into the bottom of the baking sheet and roast in a 325°F (160°C) oven until the sunchokes are tender and caramelized. Purée the sunchokes in a blender and pass through a fine-mesh strainer.

FOR THE RADICCHIO Cut the radicchio into quarters and sauté on high heat with plenty of grapeseed oil until charred on each side. Cover the radicchio and let steam at room temperature for 30 minutes.

TO COMPLETE

Warm the peas and the stock separately on the stove. Separate the charred radicchio leaves and warm them in a 350°F (175°C) oven. Place a spoonful of the sunchoke purée in each of 4 bowls. Add the peas, cooked in stock, on top and arrange the charred radicchio leaves around the purée. Finish with a spoonful of caviar and a few drops of olive oil.

GRILLED CABBAGE WITH RAZOR CLAM SAUCE

SERVES 4

INGREDIENTS

3 heads caraflex cabbage
250 ml rendered lard
150 g unsalted butter
1 kg razor clam feet

PREPARATION

FOR THE CARAFLEX CABBAGE Peel off and discard the outer 2 to 3 layers of 2 heads of the caraflex cabbage then cut into quarters. Seal in a vacuum bag with a healthy pinch of salt and cook at 195°F (90°C) for 3 to 4 hours or until tender. Grill over very high heat, turning, until well charred on both cut sides. Cut the cabbage into squares and brush with the rendered lard.

FOR THE CABBAGE PURÉE Cut the remaining head of caraflex cabbage into very thin slices and cook in a skillet with the butter over medium heat until very well caramelized. Blend in a blender on medium speed until a smooth purée forms.

FOR THE RAZOR CLAM SAUCE Pan roast the razor clam feet until well caramelized. Place in a bowl, cover, and let rest for 45 minutes. Wring out the razor clams in cheesecloth, setting the liquid aside and reserving the clams for another use.

TO COMPLETE

Warm the cabbage squares in a 350°F (80°C) oven. Place a spoonful of the cabbage purée in each of 4 bowls, top with the warm cabbage squares, and baste with the razor clam sauce.

CELTUCE BRAISED WITH PINE NUTS

SERVES 4

INGREDIENTS

FOR THE PINE NUT MISO BUTTER

500 g pine nuts
200 ml hot water
500 g rice koji
100 g salt
200 g unsalted butter

FOR THE CELTUCE

4 celtuce roots
2 sprigs rosemary
200 g butter, at room temperature

20 g pine nuts, toasted

PREPARATION

FOR THE PINE NUT MISO BUTTER Quickly submerge the pine nuts in the hot water until soft. Strain the pine nuts, reserving the water, then place in a food processor, along with the rice koji and salt. Purée, adding the reserved water as needed, to make a thick paste. Place in a jar and let sit for 2 months in a dark room. Combine 100 g of the pine nut miso with the butter.

FOR THE CELTUCE Peel off the celtuce skin and the outer layer. Slowly roast the celtuce and rosemary in the butter, covered, over medium heat until well caramelized and tender. Let cool then cut into 35 g slices.

TO COMPLETE

Combine 1 portion of celtuce and 14 g of the pine nut miso butter in each of 4 clay pots. Cover tightly and cook each clay pot over high heat for 4 minutes. Top the celtuce with a spoonful of toasted pine nuts and serve while still foaming.

GRILLED EGGPLANT WITH CRUSHED HERB SEEDS

SERVES 4

INGREDIENTS

3 kg yogurt
6 Rosa Bianca eggplant
50 ml grapeseed oil, divided
50 g fresh green coriander seeds
50 g fresh green fennel seeds
10 g Mexican tarragon flowers
25 ml verjus
4 g salt

PREPARATION

FOR THE WHEY Hang the yogurt in cheesecloth set over a bowl and store overnight in the refrigerator. Collect the whey and reserve the strained yogurt for another use.

FOR THE EGGPLANT Char the eggplant directly on a bed of hot coals. Place in a shallow baking dish, cover with water, and steam for 20 minutes. Carefully peel off and discard the charred skin portions of the eggplant then roughly cut the eggplant into julienne strips and brush with 25 ml of the grapeseed oil.

FOR THE SEED SAUCE Crush the coriander and fennel seeds in a mortar and pestle until a paste forms. Add the tarragon flowers and dress with the verjus, the remaining 25 ml of grapeseed oil, and the salt.

TO COMPLETE

Warm strips of the brushed eggplant in a 350°F (175°C) oven. Arrange the strips in 4 bowls and dress generously with the seed sauce and a spoonful of warm whey.

GRILLED FLOWERS WITH SQUID SAUCE

SERVES 4

INGREDIENTS

20 small squid

50 ml sherry vinegar

100 ml olive oil,
   plus more as needed

40 daylily blossoms

20 cucumber blossoms

20 meadow blossoms

20 nasturtium blossoms

20 herb blossoms

20 calendula blossoms

PREPARATION

FOR THE SQUID VINAIGRETTE Sauté the squid in a little grapeseed oil over high heat until caramelized. Place the sautéed squid in a bowl, cover with aluminum foil, and let cool. Strain off and reserve any liquid that has accumulated in the bowl. Reserve the squid for another use. Mix the reserved squid liquid with the sherry vinegar and 100 ml of olive oil.

FOR THE FLOWERS Mist the daylily, cucumber, meadow, nasturtium, herb, and calendula blossoms with a little olive oil and grill in a basket over very hot embers until charred.

TO COMPLETE

Massage the grilled blossoms with the squid vinaigrette to break up the flowers then refrigerate until cold and serve chilled.

ROASTED RUTABAGA IN RAZOR CLAM JUICE

SERVES 4

INGREDIENTS

FOR THE HERB SACHETS

10 bay leaves

10 sprigs rosemary

10 sprigs winter savory

FOR THE RAZOR
CLAM JUICE

5 lbs razor clam feet

FOR THE MUSHROOM
BUTTER

900 g lobster mushrooms

900 g unsalted butter

FOR THE RUTABAGAS

40 rutabagas

900 g unsalted butter

2 herb sachets (from
   above)

FOR SERVING

20 g fresh horseradish,
   scraped into small
   shavings

20 ground elders

20 yarrow leaves

20 tree shoots

PREPARATION

FOR THE HERB SACHETS Use kitchen twine to tie the bay leaves, rosemary, and winter savory into 2 sachets.

FOR THE RAZOR CLAM JUICE Pan roast the razor clam feet over high heat until well caramelized. Place in a bowl, cover, and let cool. Wring out the razor clams in cheesecloth, setting the liquid aside and reserving the clams for another use.

FOR THE MUSHROOM BUTTER Thinly slice the lobster mushrooms and combine with the butter. In a saucepan over medium heat, cook for 45 minutes or until caramelized. Strain, setting the butter aside and reserving the mushrooms for another use.

FOR THE RUTABAGAS Slow roast the whole rutabagas in foaming butter in a rondeau over low heat, turning regularly and adding fresh butter as needed, for 3 hours or until fully cooked and well caramelized. Add the herb sachets. Break the rutabagas into 70 g portions then lay flat in a dehydrator and dehydrate on high, basting with some of the razor clam juice every 30 minutes, for 4 hours.

TO COMPLETE

Warm the semidry rutabagas in a 350°F (175°C) oven, basting with more of the razor clam juice. Warm the mushroom butter and the remaining razor clam juice on the stove. Roll the rutabagas in the horseradish, ground elders, yarrow leaves, and tree shoots. Divide the rutabagas among 4 shallow bowls and top with the warm mushroom butter and the razor clam juice.

Most people that come to the island for the first time are exploring, driving around the winding roads and walking along the beaches. Our menu is a continuation of that experience, allowing guests to taste their way around the island and discover it in a culinary way.

We have one menu each night and change it daily to reflect the island. It is the job of the kitchen to pay close attention to nature and keep up with the changing seasons. It's not just about the ingredients changing but that the overall feel of the menu is the right fit, too. The colors, temperatures, and flavors of the dishes, along with the style of the plating, the style of the service, the number of servings, the progression of the menu, and the weight or robustness of the menu all need to capture the island through the turning of the seasons.

The island is so green when we start the season in early spring, and when guests arrive for dinner it is already getting dark and usually raining. They might sit for a cocktail to warm up by the fireplace, but we serve the whole menu at their table in the dining room. The menu is made almost entirely from the first leaves and shoots we find and the freshest brilliant shellfish. Nearly every dish is green with the full flavors of spring herbs, shellfish, and flowers.

After the spring storms pass and the days get warmer and longer, the fisherman go out more and the garden comes to life. All summer there is barely a day that isn't warm and sunny, so we serve the menu more casually on the patio with simpler dishes and lots of fresh fruit and shared plates of grilled fish.

At the end of summer, just after the first frost, is harvest season, which is the easiest time to cook because of the wide range of ingredients, from fruits and vegetables from the garden to wild mushrooms, game, and meat. This is the only time of year that we serve much meat. Not only does it seem fitting flavor-wise with the time of year, but this is also when hunting season starts. Even farm-raised animals like pigs and lamb are normally harvested in the fall. We make a shorter, heartier menu with braises, roasts, and larger potions of heartier flavors.

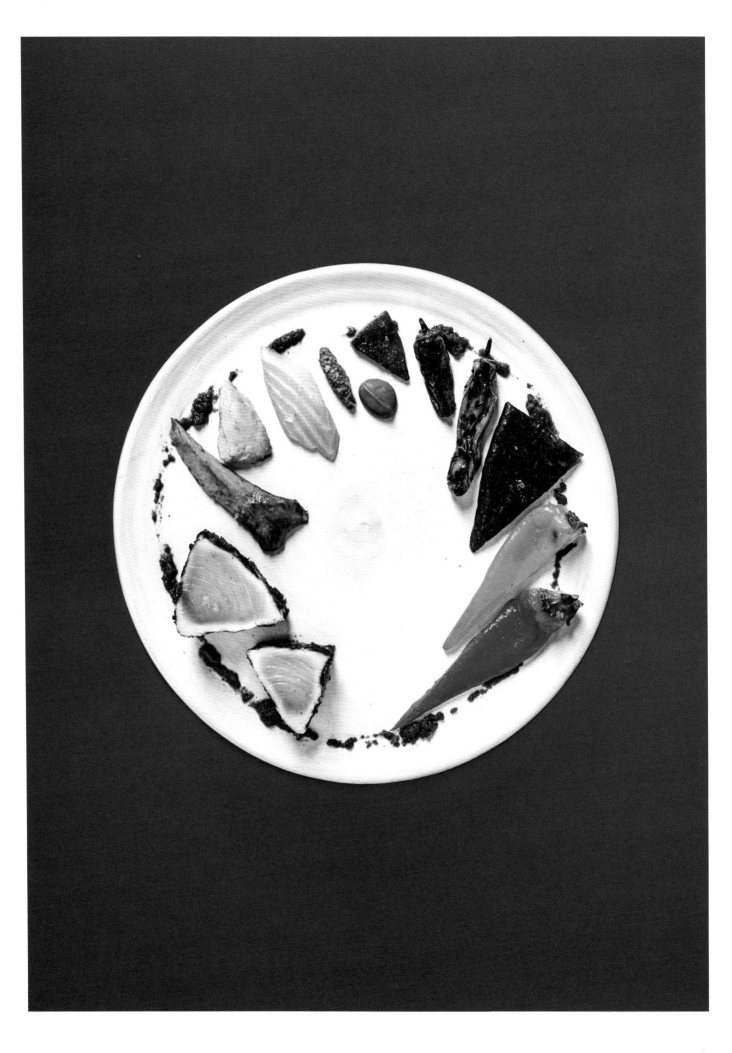

STEAMED SPICY GREENS WITH HALIBUT

SERVES 4

INGREDIENTS

FOR THE GREENS

4 bok choy leaves
4 yu choy leaves
4 giant red mustard leaves
4 red frilly mustard leaves
4 mustard greens
4 turnip leaves
4 turnip stems

FOR THE MUSTARD
EMULSION

400 g mustard greens
2 eggs
60 g fresh horseradish,
    peeled and chopped
40 ml reduced heavy
    cream
215 ml grapeseed oil

FOR THE HALIBUT

350 g halibut fillet
35 g salt
500 ml water
Olive oil, for poaching

PREPARATION

FOR THE GREENS Trim the bok choy and yu choy to 3 inches (7.5 cm) from the top of the leaves. Trim the red mustard, red frilly mustard, regular mustard, and turnip leaves to 8 inches (20 cm) from the top. Trim the turnip stems to 6 inches (15 cm) from the top. Using 1 piece of each, wrap a bundle for each serving.

FOR THE MUSTARD EMULSION Blanch 300 g of the mustard greens for 2 minutes then shock them in ice water and dry well. Boil the eggs for 2 minutes then cool and remove the shells. Blend the blanched mustard greens and the cooked eggs in a blender on medium-low speed until a paste forms. Add the horseradish, reduced heavy cream, and the remaining 100 g of raw mustard greens then drizzle in the grapeseed oil to emulsify. Pass the emulsion through fine-mesh strainer and put into piping bags.

FOR THE HALIBUT Cut the halibut on a long bias into 4 roughly 70 g portions. Dissolve the salt in the water and brine the fillets for 5 minutes.

TO COMPLETE

Poach the halibut in 155°F (68°C) olive oil for 5 to 7 minutes or until just cooked. Dress the bundles of greens with grapeseed oil and salt then steam for 3 minutes or until tender. Pipe the mustard emulsion onto 4 plates then arrange the steamed bundles of greens and the poached halibut on top.

ALBACORE TUNA AND SUMMER CABBAGE

SERVES 4

INGREDIENTS

FOR THE CHANTERELLE
MUSHROOM FERMENT

1 kg fresh chanterelle
    mushrooms
25 g salt

FOR THE GREEN GARLIC
FERMENT

1 kg green garlic, cleaned
    and trimmed
25 g salt

FOR THE DRY SPICE MIX

200 g dried, fermented
    green garlic solids (from
    above)
100 g dried, fermented
    chanterelle mushroom
    solids (from above)
100 g dried woodruff
    leaves
100 g dried calendula
    flowers
100 g dried chive
    blossoms

FOR THE SPICE SAUCE

250 g dry spice mix (from
    above)
500 g unsalted butter
200 ml fermented
    chanterelle mushroom
    liquid (from above)
50 ml fermented green
    garlic liquid (from
    above)
20 ml apple cider vinegar

FOR THE CABBAGE

4 heads summer cabbage
500 g unsalted butter
Spice sauce (from above)

FOR THE TUNA

1 whole albacore tuna
1 liter grapeseed oil
Spice sauce (from above)

PREPARATION

FOR THE CHANTERELLE MUSHROOM FERMENT Coarsely chop the chanterelle mushrooms and massage with the salt. Tightly pack the chanterelle mushrooms in an earthenware crock and let sit at room temperature for 2 weeks. Wring out the chanterelle mushrooms in a cheesecloth, reserving the liquid and solids separately. Spread out the solids in a single layer in a dehydrator and dehydrate on low overnight. Once the solids are completely dry, remove from the dehydrator.

FOR THE GREEN GARLIC FERMENT Coarsely chop the green garlic and massage with the salt. Tightly pack the green garlic in an earthenware crock and let sit at room temperature for 2 weeks. Wring out the green garlic in a cheesecloth, reserving the liquid and solids separately. Spread out the solids in a single layer in a dehydrator and dehydrate on low overnight. Once the solids are completely dry, remove from the dehydrator.

FOR THE DRY SPICE MIX Blend the dehydrated, fermented green garlic solids and dehydrated, fermented chanterelle mushroom solids with the dried woodruff leaves, dried calendula flowers, and dried chive blossoms in a blender on high speed until a fine powder forms then sift through a fine-mesh strainer.

FOR THE SPICE SAUCE Toast the dry spice mix in 500 g of foaming butter over medium-high heat. Deglaze with the fermented chanterelle mushroom liquid and fermented green garlic liquid and season with salt and the apple cider vinegar.

FOR THE CABBAGE Cut 1 head of the summer cabbage into very thin slices. Cook in 500 g of butter in a small rondeau over medium heat until very well caramelized then purée in a blender until smooth.

Peel off and discard the outer 2 to 3 layers of the remaining 3 heads of summer cabbage. Cut into quarters but keep the roots on. Seal in a vacuum bag with a pinch of salt and cook at 195°F (90°C) for 3 to 4 hours or until tender. Remove the cooked cabbage from the bag and brush the outer layer with some of the spice sauce. Grill over very high heat, turning, until well charred on both cut sides. Carve into portions and brush with oil.

FOR THE TUNA Remove the fillets, collars, fins, belly, heart, and skin from the tuna. Poach the tuna skin in the grapeseed oil for 2 hours at 175°F (80°C). Remove the tuna skin from the poaching oil, reserving the oil. Pass the tuna skin through a fine-mesh strainer and whisk with some of the reserved poaching oil until smooth. Poach the collars and fins in the oil at 140°F (60°C) until just cooked then pull the meat from the bones. Coat the fillets and heart with some of the spice sauce and grill over high heat until charred and just warmed through. Cut the belly into thin slices.

TO COMPLETE

Spoon some of the spice sauce around the edge of 4 plates and arrange 1 slice of each part of the tuna inside the ring of sauce. Carve the grilled cabbage and arrange on the plates. Spoon a small dollop of the cabbage purée next to the tuna portions. Add a small dollop of tuna skin purée to each plate.

ALBACORE TUNA AND MANY CUCUMBERS
SERVES 4

INGREDIENTS

FOR THE CHANTERELLE
MUSHROOM FERMENT

1 kg fresh chanterelle
  mushrooms
25 g salt

FOR THE GREEN GARLIC
FERMENT

1 kg green garlic, cleaned
  and trimmed
25 g salt

FOR THE DRY SPICE MIX

200 g dehydrated,
  fermented green garlic
  solids (from above)
100 g dehydrated,
  fermented chanterelle
  mushroom solids (from
  above)
100 g dried woodruff
  leaves
100 g dried calendula
  flowers
100 g dried chive
  blossoms

FOR THE SPICE SAUCE

250 g dry spice mix (from
  above)
500 g unsalted butter
200 ml fermented
  chanterelle mushroom
  liquid (from above)
50 ml fermented green
  garlic liquid (from
  above)
20 ml apple cider vinegar

FOR THE TUNA

1 whole albacore tuna
1 liter grapeseed oil
Spice sauce (from above)

FOR THE CUCUMBERS

8 to 10 cucumbers of 4 to
  5 assorted varieties
Spice sauce (from above)

PREPARATION

FOR THE CHANTERELLE MUSHROOM FERMENT Coarsely chop the chanterelle mushrooms and massage with the salt. Tightly pack the chanterelle mushrooms in an earthenware crock and let sit at room temperature for 2 weeks. Wring out the chanterelle mushrooms in a cheesecloth, reserving the liquid and solids separately. Spread out the solids in a single layer in a dehydrator and dehydrate on low overnight. Once the solids are completely dry, remove from the dehydrator.

FOR THE GREEN GARLIC FERMENT Coarsely chop the green garlic and massage with the salt. Tightly pack the green garlic in an earthenware crock and let sit at room temperature for 2 weeks. Wring out the green garlic in a cheesecloth, reserving the liquid and solids separately. Spread out the solids in a single layer in a dehydrator and dehydrate on low overnight. Once the solids are completely dry, remove from the dehydrator.

CONTINUED

FOR THE DRY SPICE MIX Blend the dehydrated, fermented green garlic solids and dehydrated, fermented chanterelle mushroom solids with the dried woodruff leaves, dried calendula flowers, and dried chive blossoms in a blender on high speed until a fine powder forms then sift through a fine-mesh strainer.

FOR THE SPICE SAUCE Toast the dry spice mix in 500 g of foaming butter over medium-high heat. Deglaze with the fermented chanterelle mushroom liquid and fermented green garlic liquid and season with salt and the apple cider vinegar.

FOR THE TUNA Remove the fillets, collars, fins, belly, heart, and skin from the tuna. Poach the tuna skin in the grapeseed oil for 2 hours at 175°F (80°C). Remove the tuna skin from the poaching oil, reserving the oil. Pass the tuna skin through a fine-mesh strainer and whisk with some of the reserved poaching oil until smooth. Poach the collars and fins in the oil at 140°F (60°C) until just cooked then pull the meat from the bones. Coat the fillets and heart with some of the spice sauce and grill over high heat until charred and just warmed through. Cut the belly into thin slices.

FOR THE CUCUMBERS Coat the cucumbers in some of the spice sauce and char on the grill over very high heat until the skin blisters. Cut the cucumbers lengthwise in half then crosswise into thick slices.

TO COMPLETE

Spoon some of the spice sauce around the edge of 4 plates and arrange 1 slice of each part of the tuna, a small dollop of the tuna skin purée, and 1 slice of each type of cucumber inside the ring of sauce.

ALBACORE TUNA AND MANY PEPPERS
SERVES 4

INGREDIENTS

FOR THE POBLANO PEPPER FERMENT
250 g salt
10 liters water
20 poblano peppers

FOR THE DRY SPICE MIX
200 g dehydrated, fermented green garlic solids (see page 150)
100 g dehydrated, chanterelle mushroom solids (see page 150)
100 g dried woodruff leaves
100 g dried calendula flowers
100 g dried chive blossoms

FOR THE SPICE SAUCE
250 g dry spice mix
500 g unsalted butter
300 ml fermented poblano pepper liquid (from above)
20 ml apple cider vinegar

FOR THE TUNA
1 whole albacore tuna
1 liter grapeseed oil
Spice sauce (from above)

FOR THE PEPPERS
8 to 10 peppers of 4 to 5 assorted varieties
Spice sauce (from above)
Fermented poblano pepper liquid (from above)

PREPARATION

FOR THE POBLANO PEPPER FERMENT Dissolve the salt in the water to create a brine. Chop the poblano peppers into 1-inch (2.5 cm) pieces, discarding the seeds and stems. Add the poblano peppers to the salt brine and let sit covered in a warm place for 10 days then strain, reserving the liquid and discarding the peppers.

FOR THE DRY SPICE MIX Blend the dehydrated, fermented green garlic solids and dehydrated, fermented chanterelle mushroom solids with the dried woodruff leaves, dried calendula flowers, and dried chive blossoms on high until it forms a fine powder and sift through a fine-mesh strainer.

FOR THE SPICE SAUCE Toast the dry spice mix in 500 g of foaming butter over medium-high heat. Deglaze with the fermented poblano pepper liquid and season with salt and the apple cider vinegar.

FOR THE TUNA Remove the fillets, collars, fins, belly, heart, and skin from the tuna. Poach the tuna skin in the grapeseed oil for 2 hours at 175°F (80°C). Remove the tuna skin from the poaching oil, reserving the oil. Pass the tuna skin through a fine-mesh strainer and whisk with some of the reserved poaching oil until smooth. Poach the collars and fins in the oil at 140°F (60°C) until just cooked then pull the meat from the bones. Coat the fillets and heart with some of the spice sauce and grill over high heat until charred and just warmed through. Cut the belly into thin slices.

FOR THE PEPPERS Coat the peppers in some of the spice sauce and char on the grill over very high heat until the skin blisters. Peel the peppers then cut lengthwise in half and baste with a little of the fermented poblano pepper liquid.

TO COMPLETE

Spoon some of the spice sauce around the edge of 4 plates and arrange 1 slice of each part of the tuna, a dollop of tuna skin purée, and half of each type of pepper inside the ring of sauce on each plate.

GRILLED BITTER GREENS AND PORCINI MUSHROOMS

SERVES 4

INGREDIENTS

FOR THE BUTTON MUSHROOM FERMENT

1 kg button mushrooms
20 g salt

FOR THE DRY SPICE MIX

200 g dehydrated, fermented green garlic solids (see page 150)
100 g dehydrated, chanterelle mushroom solids (see page 150)
100 g dried woodruff leaves
100 g dried calendula flowers
100 g dried chive blossoms

FOR THE SPICE SAUCE

250 g dry spice mix (from above)
500 g unsalted butter
300 ml fermented button mushroom liquid (from above)
20 ml apple cider vinegar

FOR THE PORCINI MUSHROOMS

1 kg fresh porcini mushrooms
250 g unsalted butter

FOR THE PORCINI MUSH-ROOM BUTTER

250 g unsalted butter

FOR THE GREENS

2 heads escarole
2 heads frisée
10 dandelion leaves
2 heads radicchio

PREPARATION

FOR THE BUTTON MUSHROOM FERMENT Coarsely chop the button mushrooms and massage with the salt. Tightly pack the button mushrooms in an earthenware crock and let sit at room temperature for 2 weeks. Wring out the button mushrooms in a cheesecloth, reserving the liquid and solids separately. Spread out the solids in a single layer in a dehydrator and dehydrate on low overnight. Once the solids are completely dry, remove from the dehydrator.

FOR THE SPICE MIX Blend the dehydrated, fermented green garlic solids and dehydrated, fermented chanterelle mushroom solids with the dried woodruff leaves, dried calendula flowers, and dried chive blossoms in a blender on high speed until a fine powder forms then sift through a fine-mesh strainer.

FOR THE SPICE SAUCE Toast the dry spice mix in 500 g of foaming butter over medium-high heat. Deglaze with the fermented button mushroom liquid and season with salt and the apple cider vinegar.

CONTINUED

FOR THE PORCINI MUSHROOMS Clean the porcini mushrooms, removing and reserving the stems and outer layers. Cut 5 of the smallest porcini mushroom caps into paper thin slices and set aside. Cook the remaining porcini mushrooms in 250 g butter at 195°F (90°C) for 3 to 4 hours then brush with the spice sauce.

FOR THE PORCINI MUSHROOM BUTTER Measure 250 g of the reserved porcini mushroom stems and outer layers, combine with 250 g of the butter, and cook at 175°F (80°C) for 2 hours or until the butter clarifies. Strain, reserving the butter.

FOR THE GREENS Grill the escarole, frisée, dandelion greens, and radicchio over high heat until tender then cut into abstract shapes and brush with a little of the spice sauce.

TO COMPLETE

Grill the cooked and spiced porcini mushrooms over high heat until heated through. Warm the greens in a 350°F (180°C) oven and brush with the porcini mushroom butter and the spice sauce again. Arrange some of each of the greens, the cooked and spiced porcini mushrooms, and the sliced raw mushrooms on 4 plates and brush with more of the spice sauce.

GRILLED HALIBUT WITH FLOWERING BAY TREE
SERVES 4

INGREDIENTS

35 g salt
500 ml water
4 (80 g) halibut fillets
20 bay leaf buds
100 ml grapeseed oil
4 bay leaves, toasted

PREPARATION

FOR THE HALIBUT Dissolve the salt in the water to make a 7% salt brine and brine the halibut for 25 minutes then pat dry.

FOR THE BAY LEAF OIL Combine 50 g of the bay leaf buds with the grapeseed oil in a vacuum bag and cook at 175°F (80°C) for 1 hour then strain. Discard the bay leaf buds.

TO COMPLETE

Grill the halibut fillets, skin-side down, over high heat, until cooked and a little charred. Let the halibut rest, collecting any juices released. Slice the halibut and dress with 100 ml of the bay leaf oil and the resting juices. Divide among 4 bowls and garnish each with a toasted bay leaf and the remaining bay leaf buds.

PORK LUAU

SERVES 4

INGREDIENTS

FOR THE PORK
35 g salt
500 ml water
500 ml verjus
2 double-cut pork chops

FOR THE ROSE HIP PURÉE
300 g ripe rose hip berries
20 ml simple syrup
40 ml verjus

FOR THE NIXTAMALIZED QUINCES
3 ripe quinces
3 g pickling lime
600 ml water

FOR THE CANDIED DWARF QUINCES
3 dwarf quinces
250 g sugar
250 ml water

FOR SERVING
2 ripe paw paws, peeled, seeded, and sliced
2 ripe persimmons, quartered
5 kiwi berries, halved
3 medlar, halved and seeded
3 crab apples, halved and cored
5 wild lemons, halved and seeded
50 g fresh green coriander seeds

PREPARATION

FOR THE PORK Dissolve the salt in the water, add the verjus, and brine the pork chops in the refrigerator for 10 hours. Remove from the refrigerator and allow to come to room temperature.

FOR THE ROSE HIP PURÉE Remove the rose hip berries from the stem and blend with the simple syrup and verjus in a blender on high speed until smooth.

FOR THE NIXTAMALIZED QUINCES Halve the quinces, removing the core. Dissolve the pickling lime in the water and soak the quince halves for 1 hour. Remove the quince halves from the brine and rinse. Place the quince halves on a baking sheet, add 50 ml water, cover with aluminum foil, and steam in a 212°F (100°C) oven for 45 minutes or until dark red, soft, and tender.

FOR THE CANDIED DWARF QUINCES Cook the dwarf quinces, sugar, and water over medium heat for 30 minutes or until the quinces are tender. Remove the quinces from the syrup and place in a dehydrator set at 135°F (57°C) for 1 hour or until the quinces are slightly dried and firm. Cut the candied quinces in half.

TO COMPLETE

Grill the pork chops until well caramelized and cooked through. Rest the pork then cut it into thick slices. Arrange the pork, paw paws, persimmons, kiwi berries, medlar, crab apples, wild lemons, fresh green coriander seeds, nixtamalized quinces, candied dwarf quinces, and rose hip purée in circles on 4 plates.

ROASTED PORK AND PUNTARELLE WITH CORIANDER

SERVES 4

INGREDIENTS

70 g salt
500 ml water
500 ml verjus
2 double-cut pork chops
5 whole heads puntarelle
780 g scallions
100 g chicken glace
50 ml apple cider vinegar
215 ml grapeseed oil
200 g fresh green coriander seeds

PREPARATION

FOR THE PORK Dissolve the salt in the water and add the verjus to make a 7% brine, then brine the pork chops in the refrigerator for 10 hours. Remove from the refrigerator and allow to come to room temperature.

FOR THE PUNTARELLE Remove and reserve the dark outer leaves from the core of the puntarelle then cut the core in half and roast, cut-side down, in a 350°F (180°C) oven for about 30 minutes or until caramelized and tender. Separate the roasted puntarelle into individual stalks. Wash the reserved leafy greens and finely chop them.

FOR THE SCALLION PURÉE Separate the green scallion tops from the white bottoms. Blanch the green tops and shock them in ice water. Grill the white scallion bottoms over high heat until charred and tender. Blend the chicken glace, apple cider vinegar, and charred white scallion bottoms in a blender on high until well incorporated. Add the blanched scallion green tops and drizzle in 215 ml grapeseed oil. Season the purée with salt and pass through a fine-mesh strainer.

FOR THE CORIANDER DRESSING Lightly crush the green coriander seeds in a mortar and pestle then combine with the finely chopped fresh puntarelle greens. Season with verjus and salt.

TO COMPLETE

Grill the pork chops until well caramelized and cooked through. Rest the pork then cut into thick slices. Warm the stalks of roasted puntarelle in a 350°F (180°C) oven and dress each piece with some of the coriander dressing. Streak the scallion purée on each of 4 plates and arrange the puntarelle leaves and pork slices in layers on top.

I always thought of myself as a better pastry chef than a savory one, but maybe that's because half of my diet is ice cream. Regardless, I really do enjoy making pastries, breads, and sweets.

When I moved to Lummi, I couldn't use chocolate, cinnamon, or even vanilla—one of my favorite ingredients for baking and making ice cream bases—because they aren't grown around here. I had to learn to make desserts with all new fruits, spices, nuts, and vegetables, along with the island's delicate flowers and herbs.

I don't like desserts that are too sweet. I know, I know. It sounds crazy, but what I'm really after is balance. Desserts should always be balanced and smooth—not too sweet, not too cold, not too sour, and not too hot. And not every dessert needs a sprinkle of sea salt on top.

After a tasting menu of savory dishes, we like to start with an herbal tea before introducing dessert. It's nice to have a hot tea to warm your stomach and make a little space for the happiest of endings.

After tea, we like to serve fresh fruit, and when you eat a raspberry from the island, you are never going to want to taste a raspberry from anywhere else. It is a very powerful experience and so delicious.

Once fruit is served, we move on to ice cream, and for us, it is important to serve it tempered and not ice cold, because a creamy, mousse-like texture is so important in allowing the flavors to coat your mouth. Our ice cream is normally served with a crunch or some type of sauce to add an appealing textural contrast.

Do not trust anyone who doesn't like ice cream. Seriously.

FRESH JAMS

SERVES 4

INGREDIENTS

FOR THE ROSE HIP JAM

300 g ripe rose hip berries
50 ml simple syrup
50 ml verjus

FOR THE PAW PAW JAM

2 ripe paw paws
50 ml simple syrup
50 ml verjus

FOR THE PERSIMMON JAM

2 ripe persimmons
50 ml simple syrup
50 ml verjus

PREPARATION

FOR THE ROSE HIP JAM Remove the rose hip berries
from the stem and blend in a blender on high speed until
smooth. Pass through a fine-mesh strainer. Season with
simple syrup and verjus.

FOR THE PAW PAW JAM Pass the flesh of the paw paws
through a fine-mesh strainer and season with simple
syrup and verjus.

FOR THE PERSIMMON JAM Pass the flesh of the
persimmons through a fine-mesh strainer and season
with simple syrup and verjus.

TO COMPLETE

Place a dollop of each jam on wooden spoons and serve.
Reserve any remaining jam in the refrigerator.

A CREAM FROM CHERRY BLOSSOMS

SERVES 4

INGREDIENTS

FOR THE CHERRY
BLOSSOM SYRUP

200 g sugar
200 ml water
100 g fresh cherry
  blossoms

FOR THE ICE CREAM

2 sheets gelatin
90 g glucose
420 ml whole milk
180 ml heavy cream
230 ml cherry blossom
  syrup (from above)

FOR THE MERINGUE

45 g sugar
22 ml cherry blossom
  syrup (from above)
1 egg white

FOR THE CREAM CLOUDS

600 ml whole milk
410 ml heavy cream
200 ml cherry blossom
  syrup (from above)

FOR THE GARNISH

4 fresh cherry blossoms

PREPARATION

FOR THE CHERRY BLOSSOM SYRUP Bring the sugar and
water to a boil, add the fresh cherry blossoms, and let
steep for 20 minutes then strain.

FOR THE ICE CREAM Dissolve the gelatin in the glucose.
Combine the mixture with the milk, heavy cream, and
cherry blossom syrup and then fill the Pacojet canisters
and place in the freezer.

FOR THE MERINGUE Combine the sugar and cherry
blossom syrup in a pot and heat to 234°F (112°C). In a
stand mixer with a whisk attachment, whip the egg white
to stiff peaks then slowly drizzle in the hot sugar and
syrup mixture and continue to beat for 2 minutes. Cool
and put into a piping bag.

FOR THE CREAM CLOUDS Mix the milk, cream, and
cherry blossom syrup with an immersion blender to
make a foam. Spoon the foam into liquid nitrogen
to freeze then break into small pieces.

TO COMPLETE

Process the cherry blossom ice cream base in the
Pacojet canisters and smear a spoonful into each of
4 iced bowls. Pipe small dots of the meringue around the
top of the ice cream base then cover the entire top
of the ice cream with a layer of the cream clouds and
garnish with a single cherry blossom.

A PUDDING FROM APPLE BLOSSOMS

SERVES 4

INGREDIENTS

1 kg apple branches,
   cut into 8-inch (20 cm) lengths
300 ml half-and-half
300 ml heavy cream
90 g sugar
3 g salt
160 ml egg yolks
100 apple blossoms

PREPARATION

Toast the apple branches in a 475°F (250°C) oven for
25 minutes or until they begin to blacken. Combine the
half-and-half, heavy cream, sugar, salt, and toasted
apple branches in a large pot and simmer over low heat
for 1 hour. Strain the cream mixture and cool in an ice
bath. Add the egg yolks to the strained cream and cook
in a double boiler (a large heat-safe bowl, covered
and set over a pot of simmering water) until thickened.

TO COMPLETE

Fold half of the apple blossoms through the warm
pudding, divide among 4 bowls, and cover with the
remaining apple blossoms.

A SOUP FROM QUINCE BLOSSOMS

SERVES 4

INGREDIENTS

FOR THE MEMBRILLO
500 g quinces, peeled and
   cut into 1-inch (2.5 cm)
   pieces
400 g sugar
4 g pectin

FOR THE BROTH
100 g quinces
50 g membrillo (from
   above)
15 ml simple syrup

FOR THE GARNISH
40 fresh quince blossoms

PREPARATION

FOR THE MEMBRILLO Cook the quinces and sugar in a
large pot over medium-low heat for 4 hours or until the
quinces are completely softened. Blend the quince
mixture in a blender on high speed until smooth then
pass through a fine-mesh strainer. Return the quince
mixture to a pot and reduce over medium-low heat until
it is the texture of a thick jam. Add the pectin and set
aside in a container to cool.

FOR THE BROTH Juice the quinces. Combine the
membrillo and the quince juice in a medium bowl.
Season with simple syrup as needed and chill the broth
over ice.

TO COMPLETE

Combine the broth and most of the quince blossom
petals in a large mortar and pestle and muddle together.
Pour the chilled broth into 4 iced bowls and garnish
freely with more quince blossom petals.

A CREAM FROM BIRCH BRANCHES

SERVES 4

INGREDIENTS

FOR THE BIRCH CREAM

1 kg birch branches, cut
    into 8-inch (20 cm)
    lengths
300 ml half-and-half
300 ml heavy cream
90 g sugar
3 g salt
160 ml egg yolks
4 sheets gelatin
1 g agar powder
30 g Demerara sugar

FOR THE BIRCH BROTH

1 kg birch branches, cut
    into 8-inch (20 cm)
    lengths
1 liter water
100 g sugar

PREPARATION

FOR THE BIRCH CREAM Toast the birch branches in a
475°F (250°C) oven for 25 minutes or until they begin to
blacken. Combine the half-and-half, heavy cream,
sugar, salt, and toasted birch branches in a large pot
and simmer over low heat for 1 hour. Strain the cream
mixture and cool in an ice bath. Add the egg yolks,
gelatin, and agar powder to the strained cream and
divide among 4 small bowls. Bake in a water bath at
250°F (125°C) for 20 minutes or until just set. Let cool
completely.

FOR THE BIRCH BROTH Toast the birch branches in a
475°F (250°C) oven for 25 minutes or until they begin to
blacken. Pack the toasted branches into a pot and cover
with the water and sugar. Simmer for 2 hours then strain
the broth. Let broth cool before serving.

TO COMPLETE

Coat the top of the set birch cream with demerara sugar
and caramelize with a torch. Put a scoop of the birch
cream into each of 4 bowls and pour a small amount of
the birch broth into each bowl.

A CANDIED PINE CONE

SERVES 4

INGREDIENTS

FOR THE ICE CREAM

750 ml whole milk
180 ml heavy cream
70 g sugar
70 g glucose
2 ½ sheets gelatin
100 g pine tips

FOR THE PINE CONES

4 whole green pine cones
200 ml simple syrup

FOR THE GARNISH

4 pine branches

PREPARATION

FOR THE ICE CREAM Bring the milk, heavy cream, sugar,
and glucose to a simmer. Add the gelatin and pine tips
and let steep for 15 minutes. Strain the mixture through a
fine-mesh strainer and then fill the Pacojet canisters
and place in the freezer.

FOR THE PINE CONES Seal the green pine cones in a
vacuum bag with enough simple syrup to cover them.
Cook at 185°F (85°C) for 3 days or until the pine cones
are softened throughout. Remove the pine cones
from the bag, cut them in half, and take out the cores,
so that just the exteriors remain. Flatten the pine cones
using a mallet.

TO COMPLETE

Process the pine cone ice cream base in the Pacojet
canisters and shape scoops of ice cream into the
flattened pine cones. Carefully wrap and cover the ice
cream with the pine cone and skewer with a pine
branch.

A DESSERT OF MIXED NUTS

SERVES 4

INGREDIENTS

FOR THE WALNUT ICE
CREAM

500 g walnuts
700 ml whole milk
200 ml heavy cream
250 g sugar
200 g glucose
50 g maltodextrin
3 sheets gelatin

FOR THE CHESTNUT PURÉE

500 g fresh, peeled
   chestnuts
200 ml water
100 ml simple syrup

FOR THE BLACK WALNUT
CUSTARD

75 g sugar
4 egg yolks
235 g heavy cream
150 g black walnuts
10 ml squid ink

FOR THE HAZELNUT
PRALINE

250 g hazelnuts
200 ml heavy whipping
   cream, warm
150 g sugar

FOR THE GARNISH

20 walnuts
20 hazelnuts
20 pecans

PREPARATION

FOR THE WALNUT ICE CREAM Blanch the walnuts 4 times
in fresh boiling water then blend with the milk, heavy
cream, sugar, glucose, maltodextrin, and gelatin in
a blender on high speed until smooth. Let the mixture
infuse for 1 hour then strain. Fill the Pacojet canisters
and place in the freezer.

FOR THE CHESTNUT PURÉE Seal the fresh, peeled
chestnuts in a vacuum bag and cook in boiling water for
1 hour. Remove the chestnuts from the bag and blend
in a blender with the water and simple syrup into a thick
paste then pass through a fine-mesh strainer.

FOR THE BLACK WALNUT CUSTARD Combine the sugar,
egg yolks, heavy cream, black walnuts, and squid ink
and cook over a double boiler until thickened then
strain through a fine-mesh strainer and chill over ice.

FOR THE HAZELNUT PRALINE Toast the hazelnuts in a
325°F (160°C) oven for 15 minutes or until golden then
blend with the warm heavy whipping cream and sugar in
a blender until smooth.

TO COMPLETE

Process the walnut ice cream base in the Pacojet. Warm
the chestnut purée in a small pot. Very thinly slice the
walnuts, hazelnuts, and pecans using a mandoline.
Scoop a spoonful of the walnut ice cream, black walnut
custard, warm chestnut purée, and hazelnut praline into
each of 4 chilled bowls and arrange the sliced nuts
around the sides.

A DESSERT OF BEACH ROSES

SERVES 4

INGREDIENTS

FOR THE BEACH ROSE
ICE CREAM

70 g sugar
70 g glucose
3 sheets gelatin
750 ml whole milk
180 ml heavy cream
100 g beach rose petals

FOR THE ROSE OIL

100 g beach rose centers
110 ml grapeseed oil

FOR THE BLACK CURRANT
SAUCE

200 ml black currant juice
100 ml simple syrup
40 ml verjus

FOR THE GARNISH

50 beach rose petals
10 g ground bee pollen

PREPARATION

FOR THE BEACH ROSE ICE CREAM Heat the sugar, glucose,
gelatin, milk, and heavy cream to a simmer. Add the
beach rose petals and let steep for 15 minutes. Strain the
steeped mixture through a fine-mesh strainer and freeze
in Pacojet canisters.

FOR THE ROSE OIL Seal the rose centers and the
grapeseed oil in a vacuum bag and cook at 175°F (80°C)
for 1 hour then strain and reserve the oil.

FOR THE BLACK CURRANT SAUCE Combine the black
currant juice, simple syrup, and verjus.

TO COMPLETE

Process the beach rose ice cream base in the Pacojet.
Place one large spoonful of black currant sauce on the
bottom of 4 chilled bowls. Scoop a mound of the ice
cream into the middle of each bowl. Use the rose petals
to make rose-shaped garnishes on top of the ice cream.
Add a tip of a spoon's worth of bee pollen in the middle
of each rose.

LITTLE KIWIS AND BLACK CURRANTS WITH VERBENA
SERVES 4

INGREDIENTS

FOR THE PARSLEY OIL
300 g parsley leaves
325 ml grapeseed oil

FOR THE ROSE HIP PURÉE
300 g ripe rose hip berries
50 ml simple syrup
50 ml verjus

FOR THE BLACK CURRANT
GRANITA
500 g black currants,
  juiced
200 ml simple syrup
50 ml verjus

FOR SERVING
25 kiwi berries
Parsley oil (from above)
50 lemon verbena leaves

PREPARATION

FOR THE PARSLEY OIL Blend the parsley and grapeseed oil in a blender on high speed for 15 minutes then cool and strain.

FOR THE ROSE HIP PURÉE Remove the rose hip berries from the stems and blend in a blender on high speed until smooth. Pass the purée through a fine-mesh strainer then season with the simple syrup and verjus and place in a piping bag.

FOR THE BLACK CURRANT GRANITA Season the juiced currants with the simple syrup until it measures 26° brix. Add the verjus to adjust the acidity. Freeze the mixture in a shallow pan, stirring every hour, until it begins to set up and turn solid. Scrape the granita with a fork to achieve a snow-like texture.

TO COMPLETE

Pipe a ring of the rose hip purée in the bottom of 4 bowls. Cut the kiwi berries in half and dress with the parsley oil. Arrange the kiwi berries in rings around the rose hip purée and add a large spoonful of granita to the middle. Dress the kiwi berries with torn and crushed lemon verbena leaves.

DRIED PLUMS AND PLUM SEEDS
SERVES 4

INGREDIENTS
40 mixed wild plums

PREPARATION

Cut all but 5 of the plums in half and reserve the pits. Cook the plum halves, cut-side down, in a large, covered rondeau over high heat for 5 minutes or until soft and braising in their own juices. Remove the lid and cook the juices down until the plums are glazed and very soft. Remove the plums from the rondeau, reserving the reduced juices. Spread the plums in a single layer in a dehydrator and dehydrate on low for 2 hours or until the skin is leathery. Glaze the dried plums with the reduced juices.

Toast and crush the reserved plum pits. Juice the remaining 5 plums, combine with the crushed pits, and let infuse for 2 hours, then strain.

TO COMPLETE

Arrange 10 of the glazed plum halves in each of 4 warm bowls and top with a spoonful of the plum juice.

A DESSERT OF PRESERVED QUINCES

SERVES 4

INGREDIENTS

FOR THE QUINCE GRANITA

5 kg quinces
1 liter simple syrup
500 ml verjus

FOR THE ROSEMARY TUILES

100 g fresh rosemary
    leaves
110 ml grapeseed oil
500 g isomalt

FOR THE MEMBRILLO

500 g quinces, peeled
400 g sugar
4 g pectin

FOR SERVING

2 flowering quinces

PREPARATION

FOR THE QUINCE GRANITA Juice the quinces and season with the simple syrup and verjus. Freeze the mixture in a shallow pan, stirring every hour, until it begins to set up and turn solid. Scrape the granita with a fork to achieve a snow-like texture.

FOR THE ROSEMARY TUILES Seal the rosemary leaves and grapeseed oil in a vacuum bag and cook at 175°F (80°C) for 1 hour then strain, reserving the oil and rosemary separately.

Place the isomalt in a saucepan over low heat and warm very slowly to 356°F (180°C). Remove from the heat, stir in the rosemary, and pour into a Silpat-lined baking sheet and let cool.

Blend the cooled rosemary isomalt mixture into a fine powder in a blender. Sift the powder into even layers over a Silpat-lined baking sheet. Using a ring mold, portion the rosemary isomalt powder into rounds. Bake at 325°F (160°C) for 3 minutes or until melted. Let the rosemary tuiles cool then remove from the tray.

FOR THE MEMBRILLO Cut the quinces into 1-inch (2.5 cm) pieces. Combine with the sugar in a large pot and cook over medium-low heat for 4 hours or until completely softened. Blend in a blender on high speed until smooth then pass through a fine-mesh strainer. Return the mixture to a pot, place over medium-low heat, and cook until reduced to the texture of a thick jam. Add the pectin and set aside to cool.

TO COMPLETE

Place a spoonful of membrillo in the bottom of 4 bowls and add 2 spoonfuls of the quince granita to each. Cover with a rosemary tuile, a squeeze of flowering quince juice, and a drizzle of the reserved rosemary oil.

PEACHES AND ROSES

SERVES 4

INGREDIENTS

FOR THE PEACHES

4 peaches
1 liter honey
100 ml verjus

FOR THE BEACH ROSE
GRANITA

1 kg beach rose petals
1 liter water
250 ml simple syrup
400 ml verjus

PREPARATION

FOR THE PEACHES Cut the peaches in half and tightly pack them into a pot. Add the honey and verjus and cook over low heat for 1 hour or until the peaches are softened and glazed with the honey.

FOR THE BEACH ROSE GRANITA Combine the beach rose petals, water, simple syrup, and verjus and let infuse for 1 hour then strain. Freeze the mixture in a shallow pan, stirring every hour, until it begins to set up and turn solid. Scrape the granita with a fork to achieve a snow-like texture.

TO COMPLETE

Place the cooked peaches with some of the honey glaze in the bottom of 4 chilled bowls then spoon the frozen beach rose granita around.

A WARM MOUSSE AND ICE FROM ANISE HYSSOP

SERVES 4

INGREDIENTS

FOR THE ANISE HYSSOP ICE CREAM
750 ml whole milk
185 ml heavy cream
350 g sugar
180 g glucose
2 ½ sheets gelatin
100 g anise hyssop leaves

FOR THE SABAYON
150 ml Pernod
50 ml fennel stalk juice
25 g sugar
4 egg yolks

FOR GARNISH
15 lavender flowers

PREPARATION

FOR THE ANISE HYSSOP ICE CREAM Heat the milk, heavy cream, sugar, and glucose in a saucepan over medium heat to 175°F (80°C). Add the gelatin and anise hyssop leaves then remove from the heat and steep for 30 minutes. Strain and freeze in Pacojet canisters, then process in a Pacojet.

FOR THE SABAYON Reduce the Pernod to 15 ml. Combine the reduced Pernod with the fennel stalk juice, sugar, and egg yolks in the top of a double boiler and stir until light and fluffy.

TO COMPLETE

Place a large spoonful of the sabayon into the bottom of 4 bowls and set a large scoop of the anise hyssop ice cream in the center of each. Garnish with the lavender flowers.

FLAX SEED CARAMEL, BLACK WALNUT FUDGE, AND DRIED PEARS

SERVES 4

INGREDIENTS

FOR THE DRIED PEARS
2 ripe pears

FOR THE FLAX SEED CARAMEL
225 g flax seeds
200 g sugar
175 g brown sugar
110 g unsalted butter
80 ml evaporated milk
135 ml heavy cream
90 ml corn syrup

FOR THE BLACK WALNUT FUDGE
7 ml walnut oil
65 ml corn syrup
235 ml buttermilk
390 g sugar
2 g salt
110 g unsalted butter
155 g black walnuts

PREPARATION

FOR THE DRIED PEARS Cut the pears into quarters then spread in a single layer in a dehydrator and dehydrate on low for 3 hours or until semi-dry and tender.

FOR THE FLAX SEED CARAMEL Toast the flax seeds in a 325°F (160°C) oven for 12 minutes or until fragrant.

Combine the sugar, brown sugar, butter, evaporated milk, heavy cream, and corn syrup in a large pot and bring to a boil, stirring frequently. Continue heating the caramel mixture until it reaches 248°F (120°C) on a candy thermometer. Make sure the mixture is homogeneous in temperature and has reached 248°F (120°C) throughout then add the toasted flax seeds and mix thoroughly. Carefully pour the mixture into a greased quarter baking sheet and let cool.

Flip the cooled caramel to remove it from the baking sheet then slice it into ¼-inch-thick (0.5 cm) bars.

FOR THE BLACK WALNUT FUDGE Combine the walnut oil, corn syrup, buttermilk, sugar, and salt in a medium pot and bring to a simmer. Add the butter and cook, stirring often to avoid scorching, until the mixture is just below 243°F (117°C) then remove from the heat and let cool to 122°F (50°C).

In a stand mixer with the paddle attachment, beat the cooled fudge mixture for 15 minutes or until creamy. Fold in the black walnuts and pour into a greased quarter baking sheet and let cool.

Flip the cooled fudge to remove it from the baking sheet then slice into ¼-inch-thick (0.5 cm) bars and place on a chilled plate.

FOR SERVING

Arrange the flax seed caramel, black walnut fudge, and dried pears on a platter.

TOASTED BIRCH BRANCH TEA

SERVES 4

INGREDIENTS

10 lbs birch branches
12 qt water
Sugar, to taste

PREPARATION

Cut birch branches into pieces no longer than 6 inches
(15 cm) and spread on baking trays and toast in the
oven until the top half are blackened and smoking (not
burning). Press the branches into a 12 qt pot as firmly
as possible. Fill the pot with water to cover the branches
and simmer for 3 hours. Strain the tea and season
with sugar.

TAFT'S BAR

Taft's Bar is a small, four-seat counter tucked into The Willows Inn. For nearly one hundred years, we have served our nightly guests cocktails and libations made with fruits, herbs, and flowers from the gardens and orchards that surround the inn.

One of the most special and unique aspects of this bar is its daily delivery from Loganita, our dedicated culinary farm, located just a mile up the road from the restaurant. Every day, the farmers harvest the season's most pristine offerings—fragrant anise hyssop with large purple flowers, bright orange nasturtium blossoms that are both sweet and peppery, huacatay, tarragon, red and green shiso, lovage, and lavender. At times, it's difficult to imagine another bar where the ingredients are so fresh, where they arrive at the door with the morning's dew still on them.

These ingredients are planted months in advance, often after years of planning by the team at the farm, the seed growers, and the chefs. It is safe to say that well before the bar opens its doors at 4 o'clock, every cocktail that comes out of Taft's is the product of weeks of digging and watering, pruning and clipping—meticulous, diligent, and focused hard work.

Some days, the bar team comes in to find the counter adorned with some of the plants our groundskeeper is most excited about and hoping for us to try. These are some of the most exciting days for us. Wild pineapple weed and sweet woodruff arrive from the garden out front, along with summer savory with its beautiful pink flowers and a flavor similar to both thyme and oregano. Another favorite is freshly picked peach leaves, which are both saccharine and bitter, and taste nearly like orgeat syrup—they're one of the ways we use ingredients from the trees out front to create flavors that are familiar in most bars, but otherwise wouldn't be found on Lummi Island.

There is a unique joy in foraging around the island for ingredients at the peak of their short season, including cherry blossoms and black elderflower in the spring, and Nootka roses during the summer months. These can be dried and used later in the year once the warmth of the season has long subsided. In the surrounding forests and along the coastlines are an abundance of Douglas fir and spruce tips, as well as white willow, birch, cedar, and madrona bark. These can be made into tinctures, bitters, and infusions once they are dried or toasted.

It is not taken lightly that Taft's Bar is within sight of the kitchen. From the bar counter, you can see the chefs hard at work on the pass, day in and day out, always pushing. Their singular focus on showcasing the island's bounty has been one of the driving philosophies of this bar program, and it is both inspiring and entirely humbling to be working and creating alongside them.

On the best days, some of the most unique cocktails have come out of this bar over the past century. At worst, it has been one delicious experiment after another. Some of the finest bartenders, servers, and friends have tended to the guests of Taft's Bar and The Willows Inn, and I feel so grateful to be just a small part of its continuing legacy. To follow are recipes to make some of our guests' favorite beverages, for your enjoyment here and at home.

Cheers!

Teo Crider

Bar Manager, Taft's Bar at The Willows Inn

LAST SPLASH

SERVES 1

INGREDIENTS

FOR THE PISCO BATCH

1 liter Miguel Torres El Gobernador Pisco

1 ½ cups Fortaleza Reposado Tequila

4 large cucumbers, peeled and cut into 1-inch (2.5 cm) wedges

FOR THE HUACATAY SYRUP

2 cups (480 ml) simple syrup

10 large huacatay leaves

4 (1-inch / 2.5-cm) wedges peeled cucumber, plus 1 cucumber, peeled lengthwise and thinly sliced, for garnish

5 large huacatay leaves

2 oz (60 ml) pisco batch (from above)

1 oz (30 ml) huacatay syrup (from above)

1 oz (30 ml) fresh lemon juice

1 dash St. George Absinthe Verte

1 small pinch salt

Soda

PREPARATION

FOR THE PISCO BATCH In a large glass jar, combine the pisco, tequila, and cucumber wedges and let infuse in the refrigerator for 1 week. Strain through a cheesecloth and reserve in the refrigerator for up to 3 weeks.

FOR THE HUACATAY SYRUP Heat the simple syrup, add the huacatay leaves, remove from the heat, and steep for 45 minutes. Strain through a cheesecloth and reserve in the refrigerator for up to 2 weeks.

TO COMPLETE

In a cocktail shaker, muddle the cucumber wedges and 4 of the huacatay leaves. Add the pisco batch, huacatay syrup, lemon juice, absinthe, and salt and shake over ice for 10 seconds. Strain into a Collins glass over a tall, cylindrical ice cube and top with a splash of soda. Garnish with the peeled cucumber and the remaining huacatay leaf.

AVANT GARDENER

SERVES 1

INGREDIENTS

FOR THE LOVAGE SYRUP

2 cups (480 ml) of simple syrup

10 large lovage leaves

FOR THE SEASONING SALT

14 g salt

14 g whole black peppercorns

14 g dried celery seeds

14 g dried poblano peppers

14 g dried dill

10 small lovage leaves, plus 1 large leaf for garnish

1 ½ oz (45 ml) Banhez Joven Mezcal

1 oz (30 ml) Seedlip Garden 108

¾ oz (22.5 ml) fresh lemon juice

¾ oz (22.5 ml) fermented poblano pepper liquid (see page 152)

½ oz (15 ml) lovage syrup (from above)

1 small pinch salt

1 small dash black pepper

PREPARATION

FOR THE LOVAGE SYRUP Heat the simple syrup, add the lovage leaves, remove from the heat, and steep for 45 minutes. Strain through a cheesecloth and reserve in the refrigerator for up to 2 weeks.

FOR THE SEASONING SALT Combine the salt, black peppercorns, celery seeds, poblano peppers, and dill in a mortar and pestle and pulverize. Store in a large glass jar at room temperature for up to 3 months.

TO COMPLETE

Dip half the rim of a large tumbler into the seasoning salt.

In a cocktail shaker, muddle the small lovage leaves until thoroughly macerated. Add the mezcal, Seedlip Garden 108, lemon juice, fermented poblano pepper liquid, lovage syrup, salt, and pepper and shake over ice for 10 seconds. Pour the drink, herbs, and ice into the rimmed tumbler and garnish with the large lovage leaf.

VELOURIA

Serves 1

INGREDIENTS

FOR THE SUMMER
SAVORY SYRUP

2 cups (480 ml) simple
  syrup
8 sprigs summer savory

1 ¼ oz (37.5 ml) Alexander
  the Grape Verjus
1 oz (30 ml) Copperworks
  Washington Malt Vodka
½ oz (15 ml) Old Ballard
  Dill Aquavit
½ oz (15 ml) Old Ballard
  Caraway Aquavit
½ oz (15 ml) summer
  savory syrup (from
  above)
4 dashes Scrappy's Celery
  Bitters
1 flowering sprig summer
  savory for garnish

PREPARATION

FOR THE SUMMER SAVORY SYRUP Heat the simple syrup,
add the summer savory, remove from the heat, and
steep for 45 minutes. Strain through a cheesecloth and
reserve in the refrigerator for up to 2 weeks.

TO COMPLETE

In a large mixing glass, combine the verjus, vodka, dill
and caraway aquavit, summer savory syrup, and celery
bitters and stir approximately 35 times. Strain over a
large square ice cube in a large rocks glass and garnish
with the flowering sprig of summer savory.

THE FLORIST

SERVES 1

INGREDIENTS

8 nasturtium blossoms
¾ oz (22.5 ml) Pacific Distillery Voyager Gin
¾ oz (22.5 ml) San Juan Island Distillery Spyhop Gin
½ oz (15 ml) Cappelletti Sfumato Rabarbaro Amaro
½ oz (15 ml) Grand Poppy Amaro
¾ oz (22.5 ml) fresh lemon juice
½ oz (15 ml) simple syrup
1 small pinch salt
2 dashes black pepper

PREPARATION

In a cocktail shaker, muddle 7 of the nasturtium blossoms
until thoroughly macerated. Add both gins, both amaros,
the lemon juice, simple syrup, salt, and a dash of pepper
and shake over ice for 10 seconds. Strain into a small,
chilled coupe glass and garnish with the remaining
nasturtium blossom and a small dash of black pepper.

WOODEN HEART

SERVES 1

INGREDIENTS

FOR THE SPRUCE TIP-INFUSED RYE

1 liter Colonel E.H. Taylor Small Batch Rye
2.5 g dried western spruce tips
1.5 g dried Douglas fir tips
1 g dried devil's club
1 g dried burdock root
.25 g dried white willow bark
1 cinnamon stick

1 ½ oz (45 ml) spruce tip-infused rye (from above)
½ oz (15 ml) Pierre Ferrand Ambre Cognac
½ oz (15 ml) Carpano Antica Formula Sweet Vermouth
¼ oz (7.5 ml) Letterpress Amaro Amorino
¼ oz (7.5 ml) Bigallet China-China Amaro
4 dashes Scrappy's Aromatic Bitters
Reindeer moss for garnish

PREPARATION

FOR THE SPRUCE TIP-INFUSED RYE Combine the rye, spruce tips, fir tips, devil's club, burdock root, white willow bark, and cinnamon stick and let infuse at room temperature for 5 days. Strain through a cheesecloth and reserve in a large glass jar at room temperature for up to 1 month.

TO COMPLETE

In a large mixing glass, combine the spruce tip-infused rye, cognac, sweet vermouth, both amaros, and the bitters with ice and stir 15 times—this cocktail is best slightly under diluted. Strain into a tumbler glass over a large square ice cube and reindeer moss.

WALK IN THE PARK

SERVES 1

INGREDIENTS

FOR THE NOOTKA ROSE-INFUSED VODKA

1 liter Copperworks Malt Vodka
15 g dried Nootka rose petals

FOR THE CHERRY BLOSSOM SYRUP

2 cups (480 ml) simple syrup
30 fresh cherry blossoms

1 barspoon Giffard Crème de Violette
2 oz (60 ml) Nootka rose-infused vodka (from above)
¾ oz (22.5 ml) fresh lemon juice
½ oz (15 ml) cherry blossom syrup (from above)
2 cherry blossoms for garnish

PREPARATION

FOR THE NOOTKA ROSE-INFUSED VODKA Combine the malt vodka with the rose petals and let infuse at room temperature for 2 days. Strain through a cheesecloth and store in a large glass jar at room temperature for up to 1 month.

FOR THE CHERRY BLOSSOM SYRUP Heat the simple syrup, add the cherry blossoms, remove from the heat, and steep for 45 minutes. Strain through a cheesecloth and reserve in the refrigerator for up to 2 weeks.

TO COMPLETE

Add the Giffard Crème de Violette to the bottom of a chilled medium coupe glass.

In a cocktail shaker, combine the Nootka rose-infused vodka, lemon juice, and cherry blossom syrup and shake for 10 to 12 seconds. Strain into the coupe glass and garnish with the cherry blossoms.

BORN ON THE CUSP

SERVES 1

INGREDIENTS

5 large lovage leaves
1 ½ oz (45 ml) Cynar 70 Proof
1 oz (30 ml) Seedlip Garden 108
¾ oz (22.5 ml) fresh lemon juice
½ oz (15 ml) broVo Amaro No. 5
3 dashes celery bitters
Soda

In a cocktail shaker, gently press 4 of the lovage leaves with a muddler. Add the Cynar, Seedlip Garden 108, lemon juice, amaro, and bitters and shake over ice for 10 seconds. Strain into a large Collins glass over a tall, cylindrical ice cube, top with a splash of soda, and garnish with the remaining lovage leaf.

LEMON WORLD

SERVES 1

INGREDIENTS

FOR THE LEMON VERBENA–INFUSED GIN

1 liter London Dry Big Gin
60 lemon verbena leaves

FOR THE LEMON VERBENA SYRUP

2 cups (480 ml) simple syrup
10 lemon verbena leaves

4 lemon verbena leaves
1 ½ oz (45 ml) lemon verbena–infused gin (from above)
¾ oz (22.5 ml) fresh lemon juice
½ oz (15 ml) lemon verbena syrup (from above)
¼ oz (7.5 ml) Lillet Blanc
¼ oz (7.5 ml) Pierre Ferrand Dry Curaçao
2 dashes St. George Absinthe Verte
2 dashes Scrappy's Grapefruit Bitters
1 small pinch salt
1 brandied cherry for garnish

PREPARATION

FOR THE LEMON VERBENA–INFUSED GIN   In a large glass jar, combine the gin with the lemon verbena leaves and let infuse at room temperature for 2 weeks. Strain through a cheesecloth and reserve in a large glass jar at room temperature for up to 2 weeks.

FOR THE LEMON VERBENA SYRUP   Heat the simple syrup, add the lemon verbena leaves, remove from the heat, and steep for 45 minutes. Strain through a cheesecloth and reserve in the refrigerator for up to 2 weeks.

TO COMPLETE

In a cocktail shaker, gently press 3 of the lemon verbena leaves with a muddler. Add the lemon verbena–infused gin, lemon juice, lemon verbena syrup, Lillet Blanc, curaçao, absinthe, bitters, and salt and shake over ice for 10 seconds. Strain into a chilled coupe glass and garnish with the remaining lemon verbena leaf and a brandied cherry on a pick.

PINK MOON

SERVES 1

INGREDIENTS

FOR THE RED SHISO SYRUP

1 cup (240 ml) simple syrup

8 large red shiso leaves

3 large red shiso leaves

1 oz (30 ml) Suntory Whisky Toki

1 oz (30 ml) Compass Box Great King Street Artist's Blend Whisky

1 oz (30 ml) red shiso syrup (from above)

1 oz (30 ml) fresh lemon juice

¾ oz (22.5 ml) egg white

2 dashes St. George Absinthe Verte

Angostura Bitters

Peychaud's Bitters

PREPARATION

FOR THE RED SHISO SYRUP Heat the simple syrup, add the shiso leaves, remove from the heat, and steep for 45 minutes. Strain through a cheesecloth and reserve in the refrigerator for up to 2 weeks.

TO COMPLETE

In a cocktail shaker, muddle the shiso leaves until thoroughly macerated. Add both whiskies, the red shiso syrup, lemon juice, egg white, and absinthe and shake for 8 seconds. Fill the shaker with ice and shake for an additional 10 seconds. Strain into a large, chilled coupe glass and garnish with alternating swirls of both bitters.

CHARCOAL BABY

SERVES 1

INGREDIENTS

FOR THE BIRCH-INFUSED BOURBON

11 small birch branches

1 liter Buffalo Trace Bourbon

1 large sugar cube

4 dashes Scrappy's Aromatic Bitters

4 dashes Bittermens Xocolatl Mole Bitters

1 dropper Elisir Novasalus Vino Amaro

1 oz (30 ml) birch-infused bourbon (from above)

½ oz (15 ml) Plantation Stiggins' Fancy Pineapple Rum

¼ oz (7.5 ml) Plantation Xaymaca Special Dry Rum

¼ oz (7.5 ml) SeaSpirits Barrel-Aged Rum

Reindeer moss for garnish

PREPARATION

FOR THE BIRCH-INFUSED BOURBON Place the birch branches in 1 shallow half sheet pan and roast in a 450°F (240°C) oven, rotating every 5 minutes, for 20 minutes or until thoroughly toasted. In a large glass jar, combine the bourbon and toasted branches and let infuse at room temperature for 4 days. Strain through a cheesecloth and reserve at room temperature for up to 1 month.

TO COMPLETE

In a large mixing beaker, combine the sugar cube, both bitters, and the amaro and muddle until the sugar is completely dissolved. Add the birch-infused bourbon, the 3 rums, and ice and stir 20 times. Strain over a large, beveled ice cube into a tumbler and garnish with reindeer moss.

SPRING VERMOUTH

MAKES 6 LITERS, 17% ABV

This vermouth is best made in a large batch and thus the quantities for this recipe are provided accordingly.

INGREDIENTS

FOR THE DISTILLATE INFUSION

800 ml Pinot Grigio distillate

50 g angelica stems

30 g sweet cicely root

150 g artemisia absinthium (wormwood) leaves

40 g anise hyssop leaves

60 g red cedar tips

FOR THE SIMPLE SYRUP INFUSION

80 g sugar

100 ml water

35 g woodruff blossoms

30 g beach rose petals

FOR THE HONEY SYRUP INFUSION

180 g wildflower honey

50 ml water

50 g cherry blossoms

20 g quince blossoms

70 g plum blossoms

FOR THE WINE INFUSION

5 liter dry Riesling

15 g dried rose petals

10 g dried hibiscus petals

40 g dried woodruff leaves

40 g dried blackberry leaves

100 g toasted birch branches (see page 196)

25 g madrone bark

FOR THE GENTIAN ROOT TEA

5 g dried gentian root tea

5 ml hot water

FOR THE DISTILLATE INFUSION In large, wide-mouthed glass jars, combine the Pinot Grigio distillate with the angelica stems, sweet cicely root, artemisia absinthium leaves, anise hyssop leaves, and red cedar tips. Make sure none of the organic matter is sticking up out of the liquid and let infuse at room temperature for 24 hours. Strain and store in large glass jars.

FOR THE SIMPLE SYRUP INFUSION Warm the sugar and water over very low heat until the sugar is dissolved. Remove from the heat and stir in the fresh woodruff blossoms, beach rose petals, and dried woodruff leaves, being careful to not include woodruff stamens or stems. Let steep at room temperature for 24 hours. Strain through a cheesecloth, squeezing out every last drop by hand. Store in a glass container at room temperature until needed.

FOR THE HONEY SYRUP INFUSION Warm the honey and water over very low heat until it reaches a simmer. Add the cherry, quince, and plum blossoms and let infuse over very low heat, stirring occasionally, for 1 hour. Strain through a cheesecloth, squeezing out every last drop by hand. Store in a glass container at room temperature until needed.

FOR THE WINE INFUSION Toast the madrone bark in an oven at 350° F (175° C) for 10 minutes. In a large, stainless steel, variable-capacity tank or other nonreactive vessel, combine the distillate infusion, simple syrup infusion, and honey syrup infusion. Add the dry Riesling and stir gently.

Using cheesecloth and kitchen string, make individual tea bags filled with the rose petals, hibiscus petals, woodruff leaves, blackberry leaves, toasted birch branches, and toasted madrone bark. Let infuse with the wine at room temperature for 24 hours.

FOR THE GENTIAN ROOT TEA Combine the dried gentian root tea and hot water and steep at room temperature for 10 minutes. Strain through a cheesecloth.

Add the brewed gentian root tea to the wine infusion to taste.

METHOD

When you are happy with the taste, rack off the vermouth from the sediment at the bottom of the tank then clean the tank.

Return the vermouth to the cleaned tank. If desired, add a little bit of sulfur to stabilize the vermouth and prevent it from refermenting or worse. Let the vermouth sit and marry for at least 2 weeks before serving.

Serve the vermouth chilled, on 2 rocks, in a cordial glass.

ACKNOWLEDGMENTS

Our team at The Willows Inn is so amazing, we are lucky to have some of the best and brightest talents in the industry who come from all over to work on this small island. My absolute favorite thing about cooking and having a restaurant is that it is a team sport—it takes a tight group to cook well and we are like a family. We always work very collaboratively sharing ideas and feedback, and so many of the recipes in this book have been conceived, adjusted, recorded, and edited by the whole team; they are the work of many. To everyone who makes The Willows the magical place that it is thank you from the bottom of my heart for every moment, every day, and all the years. It has been the greatest pleasure working with you all and I hope it never ends.

The uber talented photographer Charity Burggraaf has been a true inspiration and friend since the moment we met years ago and captures our work in the most beautiful way. She worked endlessly to create the images in this book, thank you.

This book would have never existed without Jonah Straus who is the best literary agent of all time and has become a good friend, he really helped this book to see the light of day.

Holly La Due and the team at Prestel have been so good to work with, thank you for making this book come to life.

© Prestel Verlag, Munich · London · New York 2020
A member of Verlagsgruppe Random House GmbH
Neumarkter Strasse 28 · 81673 Munich

Prestel Publishing Ltd.
14-17 Wells Street
London W1T 3PD

Prestel Publishing
900 Broadway, Suite 603
New York, NY 10003

Library of Congress Cataloging-in-Publication Data

Names: Wetzel, Blaine, author. | Willows Inn.
Title: Lummi : Island cooking / Blaine Wetzel.
Description: Munich ; New York : Prestel, 2020. | Includes index.
Identifiers: LCCN 2019035313 | ISBN 9783791385679 (hardcover)
Subjects: LCSH: Cooking--Washington (State)--Lummi Island
(Island) |
   Cooking, American--Pacific Northwest style. | Local
foods--Washington
   (State)--Lummi Island (Island) | LCGFT: Cookbooks.
Classification: LCC TX715.2.P32 W48 2020 | DDC 641.59797--dc23
LC record available at https://lccn.loc.gov/2019035313

A CIP catalogue record for this book is available from
the British Library.

Editorial direction: Holly La Due
Design: Beverly Joel, pulp, ink. with Taylor Woods
Production: Anjali Pala
Copyediting: Lauren Salkeld
Proofreading: Monica Parcell
Index: Marilyn Bliss

Verlagsgruppe Random House FSC® N001967
Printed on the FSC®-certified paper

Printed in China

ISBN 978-3-7913-8567-9

www.prestel.com